Praise for *Jewish Rites of Death: Stories of Beauty and Transformation*

Sogyal Rinpoche calls Death, "a mirror in which the entire meaning of Life is reflected." *Jewish Rites of Death* is a beautiful and inspiring reflection, offering Jewish wisdom that illuminates the greatest mystery that we all must face. With unflinching courage and open-hearted tenderness, Rick Light faces Death, revealing its power to open us to the preciousness of Life. *Jewish Rites of Death* achieves the rare integration of practicality and poetry.

> —Rabbi Shefa Gold, author of *The Magic of Hebrew Chant: Healing the Spirit, Transforming the Mind, Deepening Love*

In *Jewish Rites of Death*, Rick Light has captured the essence of Jewish respect for the body that once housed the soul. Accompanied by sensitive photographs, this moving compilation of personal experiences, poems, and practical guidance walks the reader through *taharah*, the Jewish ritual preparation of the body before burial. Rick Light is a highly qualified and eloquent spokesperson for the incorporation of these Jewish practices associated with death and dying.

> —Rabbi Jack Shlachter, Rabbi Emeritus, Los Alamos Jewish Center; and Rabbi, HaMakom: The Place for Passionate and Progressive Judaism, in Santa Fe, New Mexico

Rick Light has written a moving, important, and impassioned book on a subject that is no one's favorite. By looking through the God lens, he integrates death and life, and in so doing replaces fear with depth and meaning. He offers scholarly sources, intimate accounts of encounters with death from a variety of voices, and a well-organized, useful book for all who are planning to die—and especially those who help others on their journeys.

> —Rabbi Malka Drucker, author of *Portraits of Jewish American Heroes*, a New Mexico Book Prize winner

Jewish Rites of Death

בייה

Richard A. Light
Photography by Thea Rose Light

Jewish Rites of Death

Stories of Beauty and Transformation

Terra Nova Books
SANTA FE, NEW MEXICO

On the cover: Tallit belonging to the author's father; photo by Thea Rose Light.

Library of Congress Control Number: 2015951935

Distributed by SCB Distributors, (800) 729-6423

Copyright © 2016 Richard A. Light

Published by Terra Nova Books, Santa Fe, New Mexico.
www.TerraNovaBooks.com

ISBN:978-1-938288-55-5

This book is dedicated to my father, Mason M. Light, M.D., of blessed memory, who saved so very many lives through his work as a physician, and touched so many people through who he was in life. He demonstrated to us all how to live kindness.

Contents

אות תודה

Acknowledgments

It is with tremendous gratitude that I recognize those who have contributed to this work and supported my efforts along the way. Those who have shared their personal stories are our teachers. Through their vulnerability and open hearts, we learn what it feels like to get close to the fine line between death and life. Their holy work is a continual inspiration to me. Thank you, thank you, for sharing your experiences so others might learn.

I am honored to recognize David Zinner, executive director of Kavod v'Nichum; Rabbi Stuart Kelman, founder and academic dean of the Gamliel Institute; and Rabbi Joe Blair, dean of administration at Gamliel, without whose support and guidance this work would never have come to fruition. David is always helping me see the bigger picture in a grounded way, coming up with new ideas and opening new doors. Rabbi Stuart is an amazing liturgist, teacher, and wise sage who has continually supported my growth and helped focus this work in the right directions. And Rabbi Joe's insights and editorial inspiration have helped make this book clearer and easier to understand. Thank you, my friends and teachers. I am humbled and inspired by your wisdom.

Foreword

When I first opened *Jewish Rites of Death*, I thought it was another of those "how-to" books meant to tell the reader what Jews do when someone dies. Boy, was I wrong!

Instead, it turned out to be a gateway into a whole world of Jewish spiritual living that most of us know very little about. It tells us something about the *shmirah* and the *taharah,* the guarding and the purification that take place when a person dies, but its real focus is on the why-to.

Rick Light brings together in this fascinating book the testimonies of a number of people whose lives have been transformed by the experience of doing *taharah.* It has made them understand that when they prepare a person for burial, they are standing at a sacred moment, and that from this standpoint, they are able to peer through the curtain that separates life from death. He includes a number of very powerful poems by himself and others, and some extraordinary photographs that convey the awe he feels during *taharah,* no matter how many times he has done it.

There is much that you will learn from reading this book. You will learn that the Jewish community feels a responsibility for every single Jew, and therefore the community reaches out—first to the one who has died and then to the person's survivors—with love and with care and with devotion.

You will learn that no one is ever just a "booking," as he may sometimes be to a callous funeral home employee, and no one is ever "the heart case in Room 305," as she may sometimes be to an insensitive caretaker. The *meit,* the dead one, is a person, someone made in the image of God, a holy soul that once inhabited a body and is now making the journey from this world to the world to come, and who needs to be prepared for that last journey with care and dignity.

You learn from this book that the people who do *taharah* are never paid for their service, and they are never praised for what they do. But they emerge from the experience each time with new awareness of the preciousness of life and the sacredness of death.

Jewish Rites of Death is part of a quiet revolution that is taking place right now within the Jewish community. The care of the dead and the arrangements for their burial were given over to funeral homes when immigrants came to America a century and a half ago. Like many other practices, it was considered too European, too old fashioned, to have a place in America. But in recent years, in city after city, young people, spiritually seeking people, have taken back this "old fashioned" heritage and made it their own. This book will help these people—and you as well who are wise enough to read it—to appreciate the power and depth of this almost-forgotten part of the Jewish heritage.

I don't usually say this about any book, but I believe that the vitality, the authenticity, and the future of Jewish life in America can be measured by how many people read this literally awesome book and learn to see both life and death in a new perspective as a result.

Thank you, Rick Light, for giving us the gift of this book.

—Rabbi Jack Riemer, Editor of *Jewish Reflections on Death* and *Jewish Insights on Death and Mourning*

מילון מונחים

Glossary of Hebrew Terms

Aliyah ("ascent"): the immigration of Jews to Israel.

Am Yisrael ("the people of Israel"): descendants of Abraham, Isaac, and Jacob.

amidah ("standing"): the central prayer in the daily services, recited while standing.

aron ("ark" or "casket"): the coffin.

Bar Mitzvah, Bat Mitzvah; pl. *Bnei Mitzvah, Bnot Mitzvah* ("son/daughter of the commandment"): a Jewish male or female at least thirteen years old, the age at which he or she is considered to be responsible for observing religious law. In Yiddish, the female is rendered as *Bas Mitzvah.* (In modern secular society, some have broadened use of the term to also refer to the sabbath service at which a youth is honored.)

bracha; pl. *brachot* ("blessing" or "benediction"): a formula for a blessing or giving thanks before the performance of a commandment, or for praise of God. In vernacular use, the word *bracha* sometimes also denotes the blessing itself.

brit milah ("covenant of circumcision"): the religious ceremony of circumcision of a Jewish male at eight days of age.

Chamol: a prayer asking for mercy for the deceased. This is recited during the *taharah* ritual.

chesed shel emet ("kindness of truth" or "true kindness"): the act of burying the deceased, which is considered to be an act of kindness for which there can be no expectation of reward.

Chevrah Kadisha; pl. *Chevrot Kadisha* ("holy society"): an organization of Jewish men and women who protect the body of the deceased from desecration, prepare it for burial through ritual cleansing and dressing, and accompany the body from death until burial.

dvar Torah; pl. *divrei Torah* ("a word of Torah"): a talk on a portion of the Torah (the five books of Moses), usually carrying a spiritual or life lesson.

etrog; pl. *etrogim:* the fruit of the *Citrus medica,* known as a citron, one of the four species of plant required for ritual use during the autumn holiday of *Sukkot; etrogim* are purchased and shipped from Israel, and arrive packed in straw nests or foam to protect the fruit.

Gan Eden: the Garden of Eden, the name given to the earthly paradise of Adam and Eve; in some Jewish views of the afterlife, Gan Eden represents the paradise that is the reward for those who live a virtuous life.

gemilut chasadim ("the giving of loving-kindness"): an act of giving with no expectation of reward; the highest level of *gemilut chasadim* is funeral preparation and attendance, as the deceased can never repay the kindness.

hachshara ("preparation"): Historically, *hachshara* centers were created to train the prospective pioneers in the skills needed in the new land.

haftarah ("finish" or "ending"): a reading from the Prophets on the sabbath or holy days, following the reading from the Torah. The *haftarah* reading traditionally relates to the theme of the Torah reading.

halachah ("the path that one walks"): the body of Jewish law drawn from the Torah, the Talmud, and oral traditions.

HaMakom ("the place"): a metaphor for God, in which God is understood as being the place in which everything in the universe resides.

HaShem ("the name"): one of the many names of God. The actual name of God is considered to be too holy for nonliturgical use, thus other periphrastic names are used in its place.

k'riah ("tearing"): the ritual tearing of the clothes as an expression of grief at the loss of a loved one. Sometimes a ribbon representing clothing is torn instead. The biblical origins are found in Genesis: "And Jacob rent his clothes . . ." when he believed his son Joseph was dead.

Kaddish (from the Aramaic "holy"): a liturgical prayer used to delineate parts of a daily service. In one form, the *kaddish* is recited by mourners, although the prayer itself makes no reference to death.

kavanah ("intention" or "direction of the heart"): In Jewish tradition, actions, rituals, and prayers are insufficient without the proper intent.

kav; pl. *kavim:* a measure of volume equivalent to approximately 2.7 quarts; during the preparation of the body, at least nine kavim of water must be poured in a continuous stream over the previously cleansed body, for purification.

kavod hameit ("honoring the deceased"): The concept embraces many laws and traditions requiring respectful treatment of the deceased, including proper preparation of the body, a speedy and respectful burial, and prohibition of autopsies and exhumations.

kevurah b'karka ("burial in the ground"): Burial in this way, as opposed to cremation or entombment, is a biblical commandment.

Kohen Gadol ("great priest" or "high priest"): Before the destruction of the temple in Jerusalem, the high priest was the chief religious functionary. The clothing in which the deceased is dressed replicates the dress of the *Kohen Gadol*.

Kohenet; pl. *kohanot:* priestess

mayim chaim ("living waters"): Both physically and spiritually, water gives and purifies life.

mechilah ("forgoing a debt"): one of several prayers asking for forgiveness or pardon.

meit (m.)/*meitah* (f.): the corpse.

mi kodesh lechol ("from the holy to the profane"): an element of the *Havdalah* service marking the end of the sabbath or holy day, in which we return from the holiness of the sabbath to the more-profane tasks of the rest of the week.

midrash: a historical method of interpreting biblical stories in which gaps are filled in, difficult passages are explained, and ethics and values are instilled.

mikvah ("a collection"): in this case, a collection, or pool, of water used for purification through ritual immersion.

minhag ("custom"): an accepted tradition or custom.

mitzvah ("commandment"): traditionally refers to precepts and commandments given by God. It has also come to denote a religious or moral deed, often a good deed.

Moshiach ("anointed"): the man chosen by God to end evil and redeem Israel, in order to complete God's purpose in creation. The term also can be translated as "messiah."

neshamah ("breath"): the soul or spirit, believed to be given by God by breathing into the body. Elevation of the soul through righteousness and enlightenment is considered to bring the person closer to God.

nichum aveilim ("comforting mourners"): the practice of visiting the home of mourners during the seven days following the burial of a loved one.

niggunim ("melody"): improvisational songs, often with repetitive sounds, incorporating biblical or other Jewish texts. *Niggunim* are often sung as prayers of lament.

olam haba ("the world to come"): the afterlife. Although the concept is part of Judaism, there is little dogma about an afterlife. Traditionally, Judaism focuses on the here and now.

olam hazeh ("this world"): the here and now, in which Jews have the opportunity to live a righteous life before the coming of *Moshiach*.

parshah ("portion"): the part of the Torah that is read on a specific sabbath or holy day.

rabbi; pl. **rabbonim** ("teacher"): Traditionally, a rabbi was a man learned in Torah who taught and interpreted scripture. In modern culture, a rabbi often performs duties similar to those of Protestant ministers.

rechitzah (the ritual washing of the body): The *rechitzah* is performed by men on men, and by women on women, to preserve the modesty of the deceased. After the *rechitzah*, the *taharah*, or purification by water, is performed.

rosh (m.)/**roshah** (f.) ("head"): in this case, the head of the burial society or portion of the society engaged in a specific *taharah*.

Sefer Torah ("books of the Torah"): commonly refers to the first five books of the Bible in a handwritten scroll form.

Shabbat ("end" or "rest"): the Jewish sabbath, a day of rest and spirituality. Jews are biblically command to both "remember" and "observe" the sabbath, as it has preserved the Jewish people for thousands of years.

Shechinah ("dwelling"): the feminine indwelling aspects of God.

Shema or **Shema Yisrael** ("Hear, Israel!"): the central prayer of morning and evening services, referring to the oneness of God.

Shir haShirim: Song of Songs

shiva ("seven"): the seven-day mourning period beginning immediately after burial. During *shiva,* the bereaved family remains at home and the community provides food, comfort, and the opportunity for religious services.

shiva minyan: a quorum of ten adult Jews gathering at the home of the bereaved family during *shiva,* to allow for the recitation of those prayers requiring a community.

shloshim ("thirty"): the thirty-day mourning period beginning immediately after burial (overlaps *shiva*).

shmirah ("observation"): the act of watching over the deceased from death until burial.

shomer; pl. **shomrim**: the *Chevrah Kadisha* volunteer(s) who participate in *shmirah,* taking turns keeping a constant vigil with the deceased to comfort and protect them until burial is concluded.

shul (from the German, "school"): a synagogue.

siddur ("order"): a Jewish prayer book, specifically one used for daily, rather than holiday, prayers.

simchah ("joy"): a joyous event or festive occasion, such as a religious holiday, a wedding, or the birth of a child. Jews are commanded to be joyous, as it is easier to serve God in such a state.

sovev: the burial sheet, also called a winding-sheet, in which the body is wrapped after cleansing, purification, and dressing.

tachrichim: the traditional clothing in which the body is dressed for burial. The garments are simple white shrouds made of pure linen or cotton, and cover the body and face entirely. The simpleness and uniformity of the garments removes symbols of wealth and status, as a reminder that we are all equal in death.

taharah; pl. **taharot** ("purity"): the process of ritual purification.

tahor (adj.): pure.

tallit (from the Aramaic "covering"): a Jewish prayer shawl with fringes (*tzitzit*) at all four corners, worn over the clothing during morning prayers. After the dressing of a body, it is wrapped in a tallit from which one of the *tzitzit* has been cut off.

Talmud ("teach" or "study"): a central Jewish text, consisting of oral teachings and elucidations on the Bible and other teachings, as well as rabbinical teachings and opinions. The *Talmud* is an important basis for Jewish law.

tamei or **tumah** ("impurity"): ritual impurity, rendering a person or object unfit for holy activities until purification is performed.

Tanach: an acronym for *Torah, Neviim* and *Ketuvim*, comprising the five books of the Torah, the books of the Prophets, and the books of writings. Together they are the Jewish Bible.

tefillot (plural) ("entreat" or "judge"): prayers, any kind of prayer. Prayer is a *mitzvah,* or commandment, and prayers have prescribed times of day and forms of recitation.

Torah: specifically, the first five books of the Bible (Genesis, Exodus, Leviticus, Numbers, and Deuteronomy). Often this term refers to the entirety of Jewish teachings.

tzitzit: knotted tassels or fringes found at the four corners of a *tallit,* or prayer shawl. The fringes are made of specific materials, with a specific set of knots and windings, and must be made with *kavanah* (intent).

yahrzeit (from the Yiddish "time of year"): the anniversary of the day of the death of a relative, upon which the *kaddish* prayer is recited in commemoration. For the purposes of *yahrzeit,* a relative is considered to be a spouse, a child, a sibling, or a parent.

Preface: Some Thoughts on What It Means to Be Human

Have you ever done something holy, or felt that what you did was very close to what we know is holy? For most of us, this doesn't happen often. Yet when it does, it is a life-changing event. In writing this book, my hope is that you become open to more such experiences.

I'm not talking about joining a spiritual group or going to religious services. Instead, I invite you to explore the boundary between death and life. In the pages ahead, we will witness an amazing set of rituals that honor both the dead and the living, while uplifting both; it is a process that gives those who participate the rare opportunity to experience what I can only call "the holiness of being." It is the presence we feel when we enter into the "liminal space" that is the boundary between life and death. Feeling this, knowing this, is the passion behind this book. It is an extraordinary experience that is worth sharing with everyone, even if some may not wish to participate.

Jewish communities take care of their dead through an organization known as the *Chevrah Kadisha*. Though this book fully explains the work and scope of these *chevrot* in preparing the dead for burial, and introduces you to the ways in which we help, it does not get into any gory details. Rather, it provides an opening to the profound beauty and power of Jewish death-related traditions.

For more than a decade starting in 1999, I was honored to facilitate a monthly discussion group initially formed to explore the principles of Rabbi Zalman Schachter-Shalomi's "spiritual eldering," mostly concentrating on conscious aging. After a couple of years of monthly meetings, we expanded our discussions to include other topics central to what it means to be human. Yet, after innumerable discussions over the years, if you asked me today what it really means to be human, I am not sure I would have a quick answer. However, my experience with *Chevrah Kadisha* work tells me that one important characteristic of humanness is the capacity to show kindness and respect toward both the living and the dead.

Being human also includes striving to live the

full potential of our being. We seek to know who we are. And we want to live lives that matter. For many people, volunteering to do work that aids others, or to do jobs that contribute to the welfare of the community, adds more value to life. Those who volunteer for the *Chevrah Kadisha* have the special honor of helping those who cannot thank them, and, more than that, have the privilege of entering into the "liminal space." It is a space that includes both the momentary awareness of the infinite connectedness of all that is, and the "breath-on-your-cheek" closeness of death, a reminder that souls with bodies and souls without bodies are not separated by much, if at all.

We walk away blessed with renewed wonder, gratitude, and enthusiasm for life. Participating in *chevrah* work can be a truly transformative experience that enhances what it means to be human, and infuses our lives with greater appreciation for the amazing people with whom we share this world. It is for me the highest honor to be allowed to do this *mitzvah,* to share its blessings, and to promote it.

I invite you to join me on this path.

Jewish Rites of Death

רצף של חיים

The Continuum of Life

In the Jewish view of life, death is not alien; rather, it is a prominent element in the continuum of life-cycle events that accent each of our lives. Like birth and *brit milah, b'nai mitzvah,* marriage, and other central family events, death is silently present as a waiting partner, part of the progression of life. Death is intended to be prominently visible in our daily routines so we will always remember that we have limited time here, and that being alive is precious. Yet while traditional Jewish practice intends to face the reality of death, we are encouraged to focus on life in this world. For example, although death is remembered and honored at every service, it is not mentioned in the *Kaddish* prayer we say to honor our dead. Still, traditionally we thank God every day for continuing us in life and giving us another day.

So it would seem natural that death rituals be well established, respected, and incorporated into the life of the community. Yet some parts of these rituals, rather than being ancient, evolved over time and were first recorded from relatively recent events in Jewish history. The first written record of these was created in the 1600s, as discussed in the chapter on Mutually Supportive Death. Of course, as with all Jewish ritual, a person's level of community involvement and participation helps define how meaningful the rituals of death are. Those who attend services regularly may better understand the meanings, cycles, and rhythm of the prayers, but the rituals support not just those who practice them but all who are Jewish. They are available to all of us.

What connects the stages of dying, death, and comfort listed earlier? Why do volunteers do this? What common thread brings people out of their homes for this and the other important work? Perhaps we could say that people do this because every aspect is filled with respect: respect for the dying, the dead, and the mourners, as well as respect for the people who help out, the *Chevrah Kadisha* team members, the "caring committee" members—in fact everyone involved. And all of these people are doing kindness for one another. In fact, the ritual of preparing the body for burial, the *taharah,* is considered *chesed shel emet,* a kindness that can never be repaid.

The respect and kindness involved in *kavod hameit* (honoring the dead) and *nichum aveilim* (comforting the mourners) are the governing principles of all *Chevrah Kadisha* work.

Not everyone has the constitution to do the work of preparing the dead in a respectful manner and burying them. It is a special kind of "work," a *mitzvah* in which not everyone can comfortably participate. The emotional and spiritual aspects of these practices are intense, yet fulfilling. Usually those who are involved develop a strong passion for their work, however much they do and in whatever way they help. Why does this happen? Perhaps it is because of the specialness that is the interworld space we enter when we dare to face the reality of death and the fine line that separates death from life. Once we do that, it touches our innermost being in a way that opens us to the holiness of life. And after doing that once, we want more. Somehow we want to embrace this holiness encompassing the wholeness of life that this work embodies. So we volunteer, show up, and face our fears: fear of being around a dying person, fear of the funeral home, fear of touching a dead body, fear of being around death, fear of talking about death. Amazed at the simplicity of the connectedness of life and death, we walk away blessed.

I might note that where I lived earlier in my life, many less-observant Jews tended to ignore Jewish death rituals (I certainly did), calling them "only for the Orthodox." Nothing could be further from the truth. Jewish death rituals support all Jews, are not specifically Orthodox, and help heal the entire community, as well as the mourning family. And especially, *taharah,* the burial preparation of the deceased, is appropriate for all Jews. It is a beautiful ritual, respectful and specifically designed to help heal the soul of the deceased while providing comfort and support for the family. These rituals are based on *minhag,* that is, on local custom.[1] So every community will have a way to support every Jew. If you are one of those who are uncomfortable with Orthodoxy, I encourage you to take a second look at Jewish death practices. When I did this in 1996, I was not only surprised at what I found but also amazed and inspired by the respect and dignity inherent in these rituals.

To better understand this, we should perhaps first understand what some of these phases of death feel like. This starts to become clear in the personal stories that follow.

Aging and Diminishment

As our loved ones age, the kindness shown by family members, caregivers, and community members becomes more and more important. For those watching a cherished family member decline in health and mental acuity, the path can be difficult, painful, and sometimes harder than it is for the elder. Sometimes just being with our elders is the best gift we can give, though it often is one of the most painful for us as it heightens our awareness of their decline. Yet such times can be great teachers.

Here are some writings that shed light on this phase:

Mother at 90

Zev Shanken

    i.
The nurse explains how her other patients are much worse.
I am proud to be conversing in Spanish.
I glance at mother who watches from her wheelchair.
After the nurse leaves, Mother whispers to me,
"I think she has a crush on you."

    ii.
The nurse and I help Mother find a word.
We bend over her wheelchair,
Calling out words as in charades.
Mother shakes her head and starts to cry.
"Everybody's trying to be nice to me, and all I do is complain!"

    iii.
Her sisters, children, and grandchildren sing "Happy Birthday,"
and help blow out the candles.
While she eats her cake, we play "Our Favorite Thing about Mother."
She smiles, periodically asks for clarifications.
After the party, I wheel her into her room and say good night.
She calls me back and says,
"You have such nice friends."

My Mother's Glasses

Zev Shanken

The doctor demonstrates Mother's dependence on the breathing tube.
The staff uses the word "coded" as if everyone knows what it means.
A nurse spreads Mother's eyelids apart. Her eyes are coated gray.
I am told they withdrew her feeding tube to prevent overtaxing her heart.
"Yet her feet," the doctor adds, "are uncharacteristically robust."

They point to machines, present options. More than once the doctor says,
"There is no hurry." I recall that 20 years ago, Mother and her cousin
drove to San Antonio to visit Sophie, dying of cancer.
Mother would say, "Don't ever let me get that way."
But Sophie was in pain. Mother is dry, clean, and unaware.
My sister and I make a decision, check off boxes, and sign forms.

I discover that the hinges of Mother's glasses have become loose.
The lenses keep falling out. I ask the doctor if he knows where in Laredo
I can get eyeglass frames repaired on short notice. I drive across town.
"Is your mother a client of ours?" the receptionist asks.
"No, this is an emergency!" I stand in line, wait for them to fix it.
I will never stand in line the same way again.

Zev Shanken is a teacher and writer living in Teaneck, New Jersey. He is a member of Kol Ha-Neshamah, an egal-itarian conservative synagogue in Englewood, New Jersey. In June 2012, his mother passed away in Laredo, Texas, where she was born and raised and which she had returned to in late middle age. The severe spinal stenosis that she suffered in her later years made walking impossible and accelerated a dementia caused by poor circulation.

מלווה את הגוסס

Accompanying the Dying

Sometimes death comes fairly quickly, and other times it drags us along, forcing us to experience a journey that is perhaps not what we might choose. Accompanying someone who is dying can be both an exquisite experience and an excruciatingly painful one, all at the same time. None of us wants to face the death of those we love. And unexpectedly, when dying comes to the family, we often cannot show our love in the usual ways but must use respect instead as a way to show the dying how much we love them. This can take many forms, and depends on the awareness of the dying as well as on how present we can be with them. Often these opportunities become great teachers for us if we allow it.

Here is a story about how aware the dying might be, and another in which a tiny glimpse of life beyond death emerges:

Crossing Bridges

Robert F. Benjamin

One of my brothers was at Dad's bedside most of the morning. I was busy making arrangements. At age ninety-one and a half, Dad was starting his second week in a coma. He had consumed no water or food for days. Looking back, I realize that his professional caregivers, including hospice workers, had done a fine job of neither hastening his death nor prolonging the dying process. They were respectful of this Jewish tradition, although they were likely not aware of it explicitly.

I came to the room and suggested that my brother take a break for a snack or a nap while I stayed with Dad for a while. After my brother left the room, I talked to Dad, assuring him that most arrangements had been made but there was no hurry. His body offered no response.

During Dad's two years of physical decline, his philosophy about imminent medical crises was simple: "I'll cross that bridge when I come to it." While this credo occasionally served him well during his bouts with cancer, infection, and heart disease, it often caused him extra pain.

Then the bridges began coming fast and furious. He finally arrived at more of them than he could handle simultaneously.

By contrast, I'm the planner. He respected and benefited from my incessant planning, even though it was contrary to his game plan. For example, while at the nursing home, he wanted to go home. But his survival required the nursing home's care; at home he could neither obtain the care he needed nor care for himself without it. During his final months, I would make a heroic planning effort arranging medical transport for him to be driven home and then returned to the nursing facility several hours later. He and I would leisurely spend the afternoon at the house where he had lived for over thirty years. He beamed while in his home. Sadly he could not stay there overnight, but he was joyfully home even if only for a few hours.

Dad was a private person. I expected that he would die very privately during the night with no one by his side. My brothers and/or I were with him only during the days and evenings. We could only speculate about whether he sensed our presence. He had plenty of time to die peacefully, privately, alone.

While talking to Dad that clear, sunny December morning, I noticed his body stirring more than it had for days. He seemed agitated, yet lacking the energy to express himself more than subtly. He knew I was there. His eyes slowly opened for the first time in over a week.

He briefly looked at me. I caressed his shoulder and told him I was there for him. He looked around the room, out the window at the multi-colored garden that had kept him company day and night, closed his eyes, and took his last breath. I felt both shocked and honored by his gift of dying in my presence, as I tearfully recited the *Shema*.

Robert F. Benjamin is a distinguished physicist and a produced playwright, writing about dying, death, and burial. These issues are featured in his most recent production, Wrinkles, *a collection of plays about aging with grace, courage, and humor. His family drama about crypto-Judaism in the American Southwest,* Parted Waters, *has been produced nationally. He has been a member of the Los Alamos, New Mexico, Jewish Center for forty years and a member of the Northern New Mexico Chevrah Kadisha since its inception. He is a founding and active member of elder circles in Los Alamos and Albuquerque, and of the Conscious Aging Network of New Mexico. He has been married for forty-five years and has two children, both medical doctors.*

11

When the Veil Thins: The Space Between

Karen Kaufman Milstein

Life gets very complicated and intense sometimes. I was a graduate student working on my doctorate in human development, attempting to complete the statistical analysis and write-up of my dissertation research. My husband and I had a fourteen-year-old son and a twelve-year-old daughter, soon to have her *bat mitzvah*. I tried to stay focused and organized with all that needed doing. My parents were both significantly ill with cancer hundreds of miles away, in Montreal. We were all praying they would be able to participate in our daughter's important day.

Then the call came. My father, who had oral cancer and already had had his hard palate removed, required hospitalization again. It seemed clear that this would be his final move; he would not be able to join us for the bat mitzvah. Our daughter, Tamar, taped her *parshah* and *haftarah* portion so her beloved grandfather could hear her. I arrived at the hospital in Montreal to learn that my father was in too much pain to tolerate his dental prosthesis, without which he was un-able to speak. He was very weak. I sat with him, talked to him, played the audiotape for him, held his hand. I asked if he wanted to write any message to us. After a time, he gestured that he did, and I brought him paper and a pencil. With much effort, propped up in bed, he very shakily wrote three words: "The Space Between." He could not offer more. I tearfully reflected that perhaps he was referring to a place between life and death. He looked back at me. I hugged him. Within the next couple of days, he lost consciousness, and he died a few days later.

My family all converged in Montreal for the funeral and *shiva,* and especially to support my mother. Coming from a very traditional and formal Jewish background, where women never did such things, I surprised myself the first evening of the *shiva* by standing up with my brother to say *Kaddish,* and in addition helping my mom to her feet to say *Kaddish* for the only time in her life. Somehow, in that intense context and with our daughter's bat mitzvah less than two months away, it seemed for me the only way to confront the huge loss left by the death of my gentle and loving father.

Just a couple of weeks later, as we were all back home struggling to go through the motions of everyday life along with preparation for the bat mitzvah, a call came from a relative that I should return to Montreal right away. My mom was rapidly deteriorating physically. I arrived to find her hospitalized but in relatively good spirits despite her weakness, wanting to know what was going on at my end and to update me on her situation. She had always been a very pragmatic person, secular in her beliefs despite a strong tribal identification that included observing major Jewish holiday practices, preparing countless *shabbat* dinners, and insisting along with my father on Hebrew school for us, their children. Once when I was a child, I asked what comes after death, and she carefully explained to me that we live on in the good deeds we have done and the memories of those who have loved us. Anything else was just a way for people to reassure themselves. End of story.

So my amazement was pretty extreme to hear her in the hospital suddenly speaking, in a very assured fashion, about a soul bank where souls go after death until it is their time to be reborn. My mother was the last person in the world I ever would have expected to speak in this fashion.

I was so looking forward to learning more about her newly expressed spiritual beliefs. Unfortunately, when my brother and I returned to the hospital after dinner, Mom was no longer co-herent, and never did regain her clear focus. It turned out that she, who had never had a sleep problem in her life, was given a sleeping pill by her physician which her damaged liver was unable to detoxify. From that point, she rapidly lost any consistent consciousness, and needed to be put on a morphine drip. She was not emotionally or cognitively present from then on, as far as we could sense, and died within a matter of days.

This second funeral came exactly four weeks after the first. It was a time of disbelief and devastation, followed by the attempt to temporarily put all feelings on the back burner in order for the bat mitzvah to still happen—our daughter's decision—and to gradually reconnect with the rest of life.

Those final brief moments of real, meaningful contact with my parents, when they could each offer me a kernel of their hard-gleaned wisdom, was a significant consolation through the very painful grieving process. It has been reassuring to me that they each had the comfort of those insights to draw upon. And what has stayed with me through the twenty-three-plus years since their deaths is a reaffirmation and confirmation and maturing of my belief that, in fact, there is a special and significant journey through that "space between" in the process of moving from life to death. In addition, my knowing that there is indeed something real beyond death was reinforced by my mother from the insight she could access while journeying through that numinous place.

As my own path has unfolded since then, part of my journey has included working with people with cancer, listening to their fears and concerns, and supporting them to face what lies ahead. More recently, I've also assisted individuals and families to prepare for the special journey of the soul to *olam haba*, the world to come. I've deepened my own Jewish learning as I have explored and continue to study our deep and rich spiritual heritage about what is yet to come, and have offered trainings for others in preparing for this journey. My parents' final words to me from the times when the veils between the worlds thinned and they could tap into that mystical knowing have been wonderful and lasting gifts.

Karen Kaufman Milstein is a psychotherapist who has gone through her own near-death experience, and frequently works with patients and families around the end of a life. She also offers trainings on psychological and energetic preparation for death, with particular emphases on both care of the soul and connections with Jewish rituals and beliefs. Her work as a potter, creating often-Judaic-oriented, spirit-inspired pieces, helps to keep her grounded, and her family keeps her well focused on this world. She lives in Santa Fe, New Mexico.

My own personal experience was far different from Bob's and Karen's. My siblings and I, along with my mom, spent six weeks helping my dad die in 2001 at his home in Colorado, may he rest in peace. I wrote this poem during those painful weeks we supported him as he was dying of a brain tumor. For most of this time, he was alert and able to be out of bed but could not speak or write.

Sitting on the Deck in the Afternoon Sun

Richard A. Light

The river is shining in ever-flowing change, with clouds floating silently above in blue Jell-O.

The birds sing a symphony in tune with the wind in the leaves, as the Elder sits in his cancerous cage, waiting, watching.

His eyes glimmer with wisdom, mischief, and memory, while his body slowly ceases to function.

Unable to share his thoughts, he bides his time, smiling at each new limitation.

"It's all you can do," he said.

In grace and dignity, he bears his burden, silently accommodating the tumor's growth.

With smiles and patience, he waits and watches as the river of life unfolds.

Alert and focused, he watches the waves and sunlight as they play upon the rocks.

An airplane floats noisily overhead.

The flower's colorful smiles join him in silent vigil.

He takes a faulted step. I put out my hand—he pushes it away with a smile.

Laboriously he moves his crippled leg infinitesimally and stops to rest, trying to catch his breath. The normalcy of life is an effort—but worth the dignity to achieve by one's self.

The life force so strong and resilient—that filled his world for so many years—now a trickle of what it was, is still stubborn and intact.

He lives still. He is no object, no thing to be pitied or neglected. He is an Elder, a Wisdom Keeper, and he lives still.

In awe and wonder, I watch him live. I hold back the flood of tears bursting inside me as he demonstrates how to live in grace and beauty, in strength and gentleness; and how to die.

Each day brings new challenges, new diminishments, and new innovations.

Each day I wonder if the smile before me will be his last. Yet he lives and smiles anew.

God help me to be as strong and full and holy as this man before me, this Elder, my father, when my time comes.

Alertly he watches a kayak float by.

What a privilege for me to share this moment, these suspended days, as he shows us all how to die, and how to live.

His exhaustion does not mask his spirit as it has stolen his energy; the sparkle in his eye shines brightly.

I reach out to help him—he looks up and gives me a stern, dirty look that says, "Let me do it myself!"—I back off and he smiles.

He sits on the bed ready to retire for the night. Silent, peaceful, tired. I put out my hand and he shakes it like greeting a long-lost friend, looks up, and smiles a smile of love. I kiss him good night.

Tucked in, awkwardly trying to get comfortable, he stares into space. He settles in and quietly closes his eyes—his face now the face of one doing battle—his smile no longer there, replaced with fatigue and stress. Slowly he drifts off and his face relaxes into the sleep of the dying.

Alone, he lies there asleep. In the depths of his dreams, his soul prepares the way.

I silently watch the Elder at work. Day and night he shows me the way.

A bird sings a twilight song.

The river, no longer shining in the sun, flows ever onward into the night.

Accompanying the Dead

Just as we accompany the dying, Jews also accompany those who have recently died. None of us wants to be alone when we are in transition. So, too, the soul of the deceased wants company as it discovers what to do now that it no longer has a body.

One of the most beautiful of Jewish rituals is that of *shmirah,* the accompaniment of the deceased between death and burial. The name comes from the Hebrew word meaning "to guard," and includes both physical and spiritual guarding. Originally established to protect the body from criminals, rodents, and wild animals, the custom continues today mostly for its spiritual aspects rather than its physical protective nature, although there is some comfort in knowing that the body being buried is, in fact, that of the family's deceased.

The spiritual foundation comes from the traditional Jewish concept that the soul survives death and is aware of its body before burial. The *shomrim* are present, often around the clock, to comfort the soul by reading Psalms and other appropriate material, to make sure the soul knows it is not alone and that its journey is a holy one. Simcha Raphael summarizes this well:

> *Shmirah* is quintessentially a process of soul-guiding. Kabbalistic sources tell us that in the hours and days after a death, the spirit of the deceased hovers near the body. Reading of Psalms during the time of *shmirah* is designed to help the soul move on. But what does that mean? How can a person reading Psalms in the presence of a dead body help the soul in the transition? It's actually quite simple: Think of soul-guiding as a contemplative nonverbal communication between the world of the living and the realm of the discarnate soul. Sitting in front of the deceased, reciting Psalms, one should hold an attitude of loving connection with the person who has died. In the heart and mind, imagine sending a message that says, "It's OK to leave behind the world and move on." The task requires trusting intuition and

one's inner voices, listening inwardly for a response, and being attentive to synchronistic meaningful experiences. Soul-guiding is not a science; it's an art.[2]

The tasks of the *shomer* are to dress respectfully, show up for a specific span of time, usually a few hours, and be with the deceased in solemn respect. This is a sacred space in which chanting, reading aloud, singing, humming, reading silently, and any form of prayer are all valid ways to participate. The general tradition is to read Psalms, but there are no specific Jewish laws (*halachah*) delineating what should be done to accompany the dead. It is generally accepted that one should refrain from eating while doing this out of respect for the deceased who can no longer eat.

Some communities have teams of two people sit *shmirah* together, mostly to ensure that if one person drops off to nap at 3 a.m., the other will continue the vigil. Other communities have individual volunteers sign up for a few hours each until the entire time is covered between death and burial. When not enough volunteers are available, the *shmirah* might be scheduled for only part of the time. Some only sit *shmirah* between *taharah* and burial. In other communities, professionals can be hired to sit *shmirah* for the entire time between death and burial. Each community has its own *minhag* defining what should be done. Mostly, just having the *kavanah* to honor and respect the deceased is all that is required of those who participate.

Personal stories again help us understand what this feels like.

Why Do *Shmirah*

David Zabarsky

Despite having performed over one hundred *taharot* over the past twenty years, I have participated in *shmirah* only half a dozen times.

One of these happened several years ago when I not only participated in a *taharah* but also upon completion, took the first shift as *shomer* from 8 to 10 p.m. After the rest of the *taharah* team had left, I sat quietly in one of the funeral home's visitation rooms with the *meit* my team had just cleansed in an *aron* we had just closed and covered with our embroidered pall. A copy of the *Tanach* was available, and I invariably turned to the Book of Job, whose grief and suffering mourners have related to for millennia. With utter silence surrounding me and the *meit* I had carefully washed, clothed, and carried to his final bed, I pondered the life he had lived. Had it been a good life? Was it filled with happiness? Sorrow? Joy? Grief? All of the above? The *meit* had been in his late seventies, so one could assume he had lived long enough to experience "all of the above." I hearkened back to Job and wondered if he had performed *taharah* for his children whom *HaShem* had allowed to be taken from Job as a test of his faith. From my understanding of the book, these children were adults, but they were Job's children nonetheless. Did Job watch over them as they lay waiting for burial, as I was doing for this man beside me? Or was he so caught up in his grief and prayers that he left the task to others? Or was watching over their bodies not required because there was no fear of desecration in that Jewish community?

The minutes ticked by, and my lonely vigil continued. I turned to the Book of Psalms and read several of King David's exaltations to *HaShem*. I couldn't help but think of King David's loss of his third son, Absalom. Did he too turn to *HaShem* after he learned of his son's death, crying out, "O my son Absalom, my son, my son Absalom! Would God I had died for thee, O Absalom, my son, my son!"? The grief of these ancient fathers made me grieve a little for my companion lying next to me, and yet I had never met him before tonight.

I returned to the part of the Book of Job where *HaShem* never explains why Job suffers but points instead to his own divine wisdom and omnipotence when he asks, "Where were you when I laid the foundations of the Earth?" So many questions left unanswered.

I know that in the end, we are but ashes and dust. Still, the feats we can accomplish in the brief time given us are so fantastic that the mere possibility of it all should be enough to inspire us to greatness . . . if only we took the time to understand and appreciate the gift.

My own adult children have often remarked what a *mitzvah* I perform by attending to the dead of our Jewish community. In truth, it is the dead who are providing a *mitzvah* to me so that I never fail to appreciate the gift given me by *HaShem.*

Performing *taharah* or *shmirah* provides me with a constant reminder of my own mortality— not in mere words but in a reality; I touch, bathe, clothe, lay to eternal rest, and watch over.

A member of a Conservative synagogue, David Zabarsky has participated in taharah *since 1994. A former Marine infantry officer, he owns a manufacturing business and has spent the last twenty-one years in Raleigh, North Carolina. Earlier, he spent most of his time in Southern California. Married for thirty-one years, he has three adult children and one grandchild.*

Mourning and Grief

The Jewish life cycle includes how to live while mourning the loss of someone we loved. It provides a structure, a lattice that gives us something to hold on to when the rest of life is crumbling.

How can we possibly fill the void left by someone we love after he or she dies? Perhaps a more meaningful question is: "How can we live our lives after a death in a way that helps us integrate such a loss, while at the same time enriching our lives and the lives of others through this death?" Jewish mourning practices offer a framework for this process to occur; yet it is up to the individual family members to shape and mold it in such a way that it matters. For some, this is a private journey. For others, community participation and support is paramount.

With my dad gone, after our vigil was over, we needed to mourn, to move on. Life is that way. Yet I felt disconnected from the folks in the town where my dad died. So I spent a lot of time alone—writing. Here is a poem I wrote the day after Dad died.

Now It's Our Turn

Richard A. Light

He's gone now.

His bed is empty.

His smile no longer greets me when I walk into the room.

Our vigil is over.

His time to teach us how to live and how to die has come to an end.

Now it's our turn.

What dignity, what grace, what compassion and caring kindness—all of these he exemplified—demonstrating to us how to live and how to die, and how living and dying are one and the same.

Infinite patience, a smile always ready on his lips and in his eyes, always time to help someone—gentleness and stubborn strength; in dignity he lived and with dignity he died.

How he loved the mountains—he loved to ski, hike, camp, fish, and jeep—he loved being with his dog and being outside.

His photos shine with a love and deep connection with all of life, especially the wonders of the high country and his portraits of people. How did he see so clearly?

Respect.

I think his secret was respect.

His deep respect for all aspects of life taught us how to live as children, and teach us still how to die and how to live as adults.

Watching him die day by day showed us how to live moment by moment. His graceful acceptance and gentle smile completely overwhelmed our feeble fears and sadness. He showed us it was simply OK. Death was simply life. How simple. How beautiful. How full of compassion and grace he lived. How full of life he died.

Now it's our turn.

How to live his teachings?

How do I die living so fully, so gently, with such dignity, grace, and compassion?

Perhaps through respect I can come close.

My eye must see through the lens of respect.

My heart must feel through the open hand of respect.

My actions must be based on the foundation of respect.

Easy to say.

Such an example we have now to light the way!

How can my smallness compare to such a giant?

No—compare is neither fair nor appropriate—it is not respectful.

I can smile too.

I can aspire to patience.

I can aspire to love and respect all of life.

I can aspire to die as fully as I live, and live as fully as he did.

I can aspire.

I can live.

I can die too.

His wishes for us now would be no less than our hopes for him were when he faced this seemingly horrible time:

To have courage,

To live in grace, dignity, and respect,

To live in love and compassion,

To live surrounded by family,

To die as one lives.

So may we live!

So may we die!

Thanks, Dad.

Community Support

Where there is a Jewish community in America today, its members contribute to the molding of how our rituals work; after all, Judaism is a community-based religion and culture. Jewish mourning begins with the filling of the grave and the saying of the burial *Kaddish*. This is followed by a meal of consolation, one of the first mourning rituals just after the burial, provided for the mourners by the community to support those who need to be sustained by both food and company during this tender time. It is intended to begin the seven days of *shiva,* during which immediate family members are to just mourn: no daily job, no cooking, no cleaning, no shaving, no sex, no daily routines, nothing fun, just mourning. During this time, the community provides meals, and people stop by to "just be with the mourners." It is designed to give the mourners time to talk about the deceased and have active listeners present. (In many communities, the *shiva* services now include a structured time to remember the deceased.)

After this first seven days, the process of mourning (and psychologically handling the significant loss) continues in *shloshim,* the first thirty days after burial, enables the mourners to gradually get back into life again but without life being forced upon them. Gradually we take on normal routines: shaving, cooking, cleaning, and other daily things, including going back to work. But fun remains off-limits since we are still actively mourning. At the end of these thirty days, the mourners are asked to truly get back into life. We continue to say the mourners' *Kaddish* daily from the time of burial for eleven months (for our parents, and for some others including siblings, spouse, and children). But otherwise, we are encouraged to resume "normal" life activities. During this first year after a death, active participation in a Jewish community is helpful and encouraged. Going to services, interacting with other Jews, saying *Kaddish* with the community—all of these provide support for the mourners' return to a healthy balance after a death.

Thus the Jewish mourning process is intended to support mourners as we go through the phases of grief, and helps us adjust to our loss in a way that provides a healthy stability to life after a death. Judaism is one of the religions of the world that includes death in our circle of life, considering it as another life-cycle event that has specific rituals through which the community and its members grow and flourish.

Rabbi Anne Brener's story reflects how community involvement can change the experience:

Reclaiming the Mourner's Path: How My Rough Road to Healing Was Eased by an Ancient Map

Rabbi Anne Brener

Mourning can be a strange and foreign land. It helps to have a map. The best map available is the one provided by the rituals of Jewish mourning.

I didn't have this map at twenty-four, when my mother and sister died. In the aftermath of their deaths, I became a lonely sojourner. Horrified by the suggestion of my father's cousin that I observe the Jewish mourning rituals, and determined not to spend my life grieving, I grabbed my backpack and fled my hometown of New Orleans to Northern California, where I had once gone to school.

My attempts at self-healing sent me on a roller coaster ride through the human potential movement. I learned yoga, gestalt, and transactional analysis. I tended a garden, kept a journal, and attended consciousness-raising groups. Each experience taught me a lot, but I felt alone. Few people understood me. No one seemed to want to hear about the pain of my loss.

I reacted with embarrassment and anger. My life was unfocused. Sometimes I thought I was crazy. Was I the only one who had ever taken this tumultuous journey? My behavior, I later learned, was exactly like a mourner's. And the rough path toward healing was known, and the journey had been eased centuries ago, by the rabbis who created the rituals of mourning.

Twenty years later, my reaction to my father's death was profoundly different, because I had this map. Upon receiving the news of his death, I ripped my garment and recited the blessing praising "God the true judge." Then I called my father's rabbi in New Orleans and made certain that members of his congregation would perform the sacred duty of sitting with my dad's body, reciting psalms until I could get there from Los Angeles and say my final goodbye.

After the funeral, I knew how to accept the congregation's generosity. The people who had stood in prayer with my father over the course of his lifetime came to sit with me in his apartment during *shiva*. Twice a day for seven days, they came, offering food and prayer until I found my own voice in the words of the *Kaddish* and could return to my home in Los Angeles to say the mourner's prayer on my own.

When the week of *shiva* ended, I followed the tradition of walking around the block to reenter the world, accompanied by members of my father's community. Strengthened by their caring and compassion, I was able to leave his house and return to Los Angeles, where I would walk the less-protected path of the first year of mourning.

During that time, my own synagogue community held a place for me where I could regularly recite the *Kaddish*. The word "place" is of great significance; it is the name used for God— *HaMakom*, the Place. When the Temple stood in Jerusalem, mourners had a place—a separate gate through which they entered and continued walking along a special Mourner's Path. As they walked, they came face to face with all the other members of the community, who greeted them with the blessing, "May the One who dwells in this place comfort you. May you find God— *HaMakom*—the holy place of comfort."

Those walking in the opposite direction, former mourners who had made it through, affirmed by their presence the possibility of healing. Looking into their experienced eyes, the mourners found comfort in the knowledge that one does not walk the Mourner's Path forever.

Those who had never walked the Mourner's Path looked into the face of grief and learned that death and loss are part of life. Knowing that someday, they too would walk this path, they could prepare themselves for that eventuality. They realized also that when that day came, they would not be alone; they would walk in the company of other survivors.

When the Temple stood, the commonality of the various experiences of loss was publicly acknowledged. Others joined the mourners on the path. For it was understood that economic reverses, personal illness, relocation, and the illness of someone close required attention similar to that given to mourners. As it says in the Talmud: "Who are they who circle to the left? A mourner, an excommunicant, one who has someone sick at home, and one concerned about a lost object" (Minor Tractate of Talmud: *Semachot*).

The existence of the Mourner's Path confirmed that it is acceptable for those facing significant loss to be out of step with others, and affirmed their status as a normal part of community life. Having their experience mirrored in this holy place kept mourners from feeling invisible, unsupported, or ashamed.

Today, we do not have such places. We no longer live in small communities that share our sorrow. More often than not, we attend funerals out of state and then hurry home to a transitory community where few people share our grief. When no one around us carries the stories and memories that mirror our loss and bring us comfort, our pain becomes even more invisible. Moreover, death is often seen in our society as a failure of the medical community, something abnormal and inappropriate. The bereaved are not encouraged to take time out to walk the Mourner's Path. Having a strong reaction to a death, one that prevents the mourner from bouncing back into the normal stream of living, is seen as evidence of maladjustment, requiring the help of psychiatrists or social workers. *HaMakom* is hard to find.

How then do we reclaim the Mourner's Path for the Jewish community and remove the negative connotations associated with this universal experience?

After returning to Los Angeles at the end of *shiva,* I continued to wear the cut black ribbon given to me at the funeral. It was the only visible sign of the profound change in my life. This practice has roots in the Jewish tradition of *k'riah,* in which a person rips her or his garment upon hearing of the death of someone she or he will mourn. As it says in the *Shulchan Aruch,* ". . . all garments must be rent opposite the heart . . . for the mourner has to expose the heart" (*Kitzur Shulchan Aruch*: 195:3–4).

After the completion of *shloshim,* the first month of mourning, I was reluctant to remove the ribbon, not wanting to hide my heart. I had appreciated the compassionate nods of recognition I received from those who understood the significance of my little ribbon. Their silent deference, their awareness of my status as a mourner, continued to provide reassurance, to help me stay connected to my feelings and focus on my grief work. I felt acknowledged as one walking an ancient and venerable path. Gone was the shame and embarrassment I had felt twenty years earlier.

Rather than surrender my ribbon, I decided to embrace it and reclaim the visibility of mourning. I began handing out colored ribbons to signify the varying status of those who walk the Mourner's Path: black ribbons in the first year of mourning; green ribbons for those observing a *yahrzeit* or other significant date connected to a loss; blue ribbons for people in the midst of other major life changes such as divorce, ending a relationship, relocation, change of job, illness, or becoming a caretaker for someone who is ill; and purple ribbons for those whose lives have been transformed by the journey of mourning.

Wearing these visible marks of mourning helps guide the process of healing. Some people will bring comfort through gently acknowledging the significance of the ribbon. Others may ask the ribbon's meaning and give the mourner a chance to tell his or her story. All of these responses give the bereaved validation and solace.

Ironically, being marked as different makes it easier for the mourner to return to the mundane tasks of everyday living. Visible ribbons give mourners relief from the incongruity they feel when their inner experience of grief is masked by the persona they feel obliged to present to a community that is unaware of their loss. Without the burden of covering up their sense of brokenness, mourners are able to attend to their deeper emotional and spiritual needs.

After a while, people begin playing with the ribbons. They weave them into their jewelry, wrap them around their buttons, and finger them as comforting talismans. In those actions, the experience of mourning begins to change. It shifts from a static state to an active, creative process—a kind of dance.

Indeed, mourning is a dance. It is a dance that has been choreographed over the millennia by everyone who has passed through the Mourner's Path. By making loss and bereavement visible, we can fulfill the psalmist's promise: to turn mourning into dancing.

Reprinted with permission from *Reform Judaism* magazine (reformjudaismmag.org), published by the Union for Reform Judaism.

Rabbi Anne Brener, LCSW, is a Los Angeles based psychotherapist and spiritual director and a frequent scholar-in-residence who has assisted institutions from Brazil to Israel and Africa and throughout North America in creating caring communities. She is a frequent columnist for the Los Angeles Jewish Journal. *Her work has been translated into Portuguese, Spanish, and several African dialects. Ordained as a Reform rabbi in 2008, she is also a graduate of Hebrew Union College's School of Communal Service, the University of Southern California's School of Social Work, and San Francisco State University's Department of Broadcast Communication Arts.*

נשמת אפו של העניין

The Soul of the Matter

Jewish death practices have a number of under-lying principles that glue everything together. One of those is the essential Jewish concept that we each have a soul. It is based on the hope that life matters in part because we live on afterward in some nonphysical form. What we do to help the dead is directly related to what we believe about the soul, life after death, and the fact that respect for ho-liness is important. To truly understand *taharah*, one must first understand the soul's role in all of this.

A Jewish View of Soul

One of the major underlying principles that supports and guides the work of the *Chevrah Kadisha* is the Jewish belief that each individual is composed of both physical and nonphysical elements, a body and a soul, with the soul (*neshamah*) as the eternal, nonphysical, spiritual aspect of each human being that lives on after the death of the body.[3] It is the part that stays alive when we die. Pierre Teilhard de Chardin, the noted French philosopher, paleontologist, geologist, and Jesuit priest, said: "We are not human beings having a spiritual experience. We are spiritual beings having a human experience." We can think of our life here on Earth perhaps as a short class taken by our soul at the earthly community college. The physical life that we know is the transitory part, while the soul-level, nonphysical, spiritual life is the permanent aspect of who we are.

"Soul" is hard to define exactly. There are many Jewish views on exactly what the soul is. Among other terms, it has been described as the essence of our being, an individual extension of God, the divine spark that animates us, the nonphysical aspect of ourselves that connects us to the whole of life, our inner self, and the core within that harbors our awareness. The common threads in these descriptions include the ideas that soul is intangible, eternal,[4] not physically measurable, connected with our being alive and breathing, and has divine characteristics. Jews traditionally believe there is a soul, a divine essence that inhabits, animates, and gives life to the body, and that this part of us is aware during life and lives on after death. In Jewish mystical tradition, the soul also connects us directly to the source of creation. Rabbi Elie Kaplan Spitz writes:

> Characterizing soul as an extension of God helps me appreciate why soul is so hard to define. God is *other,* neither object nor person. To experience God and soul entails some detachment from our own self-involvement, our "I." The image of soul as breath helps convey a paradox. Although we don't normally see our breath, if we take a mirror, breathe in deeply, and exhale, we can see our breath as film on the mirror. The more

breath we see, the less reflection we see of ourselves. To define objects is to grasp them with our senses, which requires an awareness of ourselves. The more fully we encounter soul, the more our "I" of self-awareness and attachment recedes. We engage soul with the aid of our imagination.[5]

Rabbi Spitz documents near-death experiences that describe deceased relatives waiting on the other side, relatives seemingly "alive and well" but in a nonphysical form. Those who had near-death experiences also had the experience of awareness outside the body that was independent of the body, observing what happened while they were "dead."[6] In well-known mystical writings, there are descriptions of deceased masters or relatives who speak to the living after the master or relative has died. Even in our modern age, there are psychics who channel the dead, describing in great detail information that the psychic person could not have known.[7] All of these point to the existence and acknowledgement of life beyond the physical. These experiences describe the soul living on after death and remembering its previous life and the people involved in that life.

One day in 1999, while driving from Colorado back to New Mexico with two ten-year-olds in the back seat, I approached the only traffic light in the small town of Tres Piedras, flashing red in one direction and yellow in the other. Drivers on the side street are to stop, and those on the main road, as I was, should proceed. I was carefully obeying the speed limit, gliding along at 45 MPH, not expecting to stop as I listened to a book on tape about near-death experiences. As I approached the flashing yellow light, I noticed out of the corner of my eye a white, box-shaped van approaching from my left—moving extremely fast. Suddenly it dawned on me that it was not going to stop, and I was already in the intersection!

Before I could even respond, I found myself high above my body, observing all that was happening. Time morphed to a crawl as everything proceeded in slow motion. I was calm, relaxed, present, watching. The van was crossing just ahead of my front bumper, inches away, like a ghost in the night, ever so imperceptibly progressing across the intersection with my bumper getting ever closer to hitting it. I saw my leg extend, the brake push down, the car slow in response. Silently the van inched across the intersection. As its back bumper cleared my right headlight, everything suddenly zoomed back into real time! In an instant, I was back in my body, the van disappearing off to the right as we flew through the intersection. As the voice on the tape continued to describe "out-of-body experiences," I pulled over to breathe and come to terms with what just happened.

What part of me was watching? Was it my soul? Where was "I" in all of this?

One of the central teachings that caught my attention back in 1971 when I began studying East Indian meditation and Vedic teachings about consciousness is the concept of "witnessing." The idea is that we are consciousness inhabiting a body, and as such, we are intelligence that is aware of itself. Hence, if we are fully awake in our lives, we can be aware of our being witnessing our own actions as we live our lives. As I sat there trembling on the side of the road, one of the kids in the back seat reminded me that we had just had a "near-death experience"! It was not quite the same as those on the tape, but "near-death" just the same. I had experienced being the witness.

For many years now, I have been fortunate to help prepare Jewish bodies for burial. When I work with the dead, I often feel their presence in the room. It feels like their soul is hovering around their now-empty body, fully aware of what we are doing, and often very appreciative of our work. I can feel the gratitude in the room. So when I think of what I experienced back at that intersection, I wonder if I was looking through the eyes of my soul.

When my dad died in 2001, I was devastated. May his memory be a blessing. I cherished him and respected him beyond most men in the world. He was a physician and surgeon in a small town in Colorado, and although he was not very religious, he was what I would call quite spiritual in his living. A few days after his death, I foolishly thought that since I had studied Judaism and other religions and felt close to God, and since he was not religious and I was, I should remind him to look for God. So I went out on the porch and said in a sort of undertone, "Dad, maybe if you look around, you will find God." Immediately, there came this voice inside me, strong and calm, loud and clear: "You find God in your own heart!" It felt like a bolt of lightning had just struck me! I had to humble myself and realize that not only was Dad right but he was still aware and still "alive" on some level, still around. He was talking to me, and I was not "the one who knows more than he does" as I had thought I was! Once again, I got to experience a soul-level event. Thank you, Dad, for humbling me and for teaching me even after death.

נוגע בצעיף בין העולמות

Touching the Veil Between Worlds

It all started in 1952. I was two at the time, walking down the hallway of my family home in Gunnison, Colorado. As I looked at the plain white wall, I suddenly saw a vision of myself as an adult. I saw my adult face accompanied by an overwhelming sense of sadness and loss. I had the gut realization that I was stuck in a limited physical body with that face and curly hair—and I was no longer boundless.

Only as an adult did I understand what I had seen and experienced. Later, as I learned about souls and spiritual things, and subsequently got into *Chevrah Kadisha* work, it dawned on me that my experience was another soul event. This was the realization by my soul that it was no longer an unfettered, unbounded being; rather, it now was contained in an earthly vessel, and the joy and freedom of nonphysical life was being somehow "lost" or put on hold while I was here. This was the sadness accompanying my vision.

The basic premise when a *chevrah* team walks in to do *taharah* is that the soul of the deceased is in the room with them, watching, aware, interested in what's going on with its now-detached body.

Everything the *chevrah* does is related to this idea. Sometimes, we are aware of the soul in the room, and sometimes we are not. Yet everything we do assumes the soul is there.

The more I learn about preparing Jewish bodies for burial, and the concept of souls living on after death, the more I am inspired to do *Chevrah Kadisha* work. I am thrilled to help out, to make a difference, to do something of real value. For me, each *taharah* is an unparalleled opportunity to help someone move from one divine realm of existence to another. How often do we get to do that in our daily lives?

My experience of the power of *taharah* to connect to other realms comes from my first introduction to this work. There I was, at forty-six years old, lying on the table, dead. Six intensely focused people were huddled around me reciting specific liturgy from scripture and dressing me in burial shrouds. Not knowing how to be dead, I tried to just be "dead weight," loose, relaxed, and present. As I followed their progress, I soon found myself in a bright, white light. I was gone. All that existed for me was the light. That's the only thing I could see, hear, feel, experience. Time stopped. Place stopped. Voices stopped. Life stopped. I was suspended in pure, brilliant "beingness"—aware but not limited in time, space, or personality.

Earlier that week in the spring of 1996, a friend who was our "lay rabbi" at the local *shul* had called suggesting that I attend a training in a nearby city about an "esoteric side of Judaism that we should check out to see if we want to do it here." He had asked me to go because I was the only Jew he knew who was into "weird spiritual things." It turned out to be training for the *Chevrah Kadisha.* We had a verbal training in the morning. Now, we were doing a role-play experiential training in which the team practiced the entire procedure of the *taharah,* the ritual of washing and dressing the dead. Luckily, the members were only simulating the washing of the body and the spiritual pouring of water, since I was, after all, not really dead.

Suddenly, I was "awakened" by one of the team.

I slowly opened my eyes and tried to adjust to the real world again. Someone said, "We could tell by the look on your face that you were somewhere else!" Where I went and what happened to me there are still unexplained phenomena. When I described what had happened, everyone was amazed, including me. It was an extraordinary experience for all of us, so much so that I returned home to start a local *Chevrah Kadisha.* If a dry run could be so transformative, how much more powerful must be the real thing!

Each time my local *chevrah* is called, we hold a short briefing for the members of the team before and after the *taharah* itself, to make sure everyone on the team is emotionally and physically healthy. During the debriefing after a *taharah* I led in 2011, an experienced member of our *chevrah* mentioned to a newer member that he hoped when we next met it would be under better circumstances. The response from the new member inspired this poem:

Sacred Undertaking

Richard A. Light

Sacred Undertaking . . . today I midwifed a soul from this world to the next.
The call came in; assembled the team.
Set intentions to see God's face in the deceased and in each other.

Entered in silence.
He didn't look so good on the table.
Closed his lifeless eyes, covered his nakedness.
Spoke softly.
Read from the Song of Songs.
Carefully washed his body, head to toe, respecting his modesty and dignity.
It was tricky to wash his back.
Trimmed his fingernails, cleaned him up.
New dry sheet covering him now.

Quoted Rabbi Akiva, "You are fortunate Israel . . . I will purify you."
Poured the living waters. *"Tahor hu, tahor hu, tahor hu!"* He is pure.
Dried his body.

Dressed him as the High Priest; the name of the Holy One tied into the knots.
Laid him gently into the waiting coffin sprinkled with holy earth from Israel.
More readings. More silence.
Asked for forgiveness in case we did not show enough respect.

Then it was again obvious—then it was that I noticed how he radiated the Light.
I had seen it before. The Radiance. The Grace.

His gratitude was palpable.

Sacred Undertaking … today I midwifed a soul from this world to the next.
Today, I was reminded.

Someone said, "I hope we meet again under better circumstances."
The reply was, "These are the most holy of circumstances. These are the best circumstances."
Today, I was reminded.

Sacred Undertaking . . .
Today, I midwifed a soul from this world to the next.
Today, I was blessed.

Midwifing a Soul

Have you ever witnessed a midwife bringing a baby into the world? It's an amazing event. And what does the midwife do? Generally, she guides those involved, supports them, and helps them feel calm as they go through a transition. She helps them feel safe. And now for a minute, think about the child being born. It's a hard transition for the child: from a dark, warm, water-filled world that is safe and known into a brightly lit, cold, air-filled world that is very strange and unknown.

I might suggest that when we die, we are going through a parallel process: from a known world that is physical and navigated using a vehicle called the body to a strange and unknown world that is non-physical and has no body. To the higher aspects of our soul, this realm is familiar, but to the part of our soul that is our conscious personality in this life, the new realm is unfamiliar. Wouldn't it be nice to have a midwife to ease our way as we go through the death transition? Let's explore what it takes to midwife a soul from one realm of existence to another, from the *olam hazeh* (this physical world) to the *olam haba* (the unseen spiritual world). To do this we must examine what it feels like to face the reality of death, to do holy work for which no one can thank you, to know what it is to help a soul outside its body move between realms. And to do this, one must enter into the liminal space: the boundary where death and life meet.

Taharah *Experiences*

The idea of midwifing a soul from this world to another is truly foreign to most of us. It seems esoteric, strange, somehow out of our reach, and certainly not something most of us can relate to. Everyone feels and experiences different things doing this work. There are no right or wrong experiences. Everything experienced is a valid part of the continuum that is the *Chevrah Kadisha* world. Every *taharah* is different. Every team member experiences different things, even in the same *taharah*.

So how can I share with you what it is like to participate in this holy work? If I ask you to describe what cinnamon tastes like to someone who has never tasted it, what would you say? Similarly, I cannot give you the experience of touching the veil, but I can share stories of those who have done it, as they describe in their own words what they felt and experienced.

This is a collection of stories of *taharah* experiences from everyday people who are involved in this work. Each story includes something very special.

The Greatest *Mitzvah*

Mildred L. Covert

As a member of the New Orleans *Chevrah Kadisha,* I am often asked: "Why do you do this?" "How can you do this?" "Isn't it depressing to deal with death?" "How did you get involved?"

Knowing what the *Chevrah Kadisha* is and what it does is paramount to understanding the answers.

Not many Jews are aware of the role of the *Chevrah Kadisha,* and, in fact, because it has to do with the dead, information about it, even when available, is avoided. Yet it is a beautiful aspect of Jewish life, and if any one *mitzvah* displays the highest level of Jewish practice, perhaps the work of the *Chevrah Kadisha* is it.

Throughout Jewish history, communities the world over established burial societies whose sole function was the care of the deceased from the time of death until interment. This was done to ensure dignified treatment of the deceased in accordance with Jewish law, custom, and tradition.

The *Chevrah Kadisha* is comprised of dedicated men and women who perform the most sacred of Jewish rituals, the *taharah,* before interment. During the process, as Judaism requires, we treat every human being with dignity and respect. The men prepare the males, and women prepare the females.

This ritual of *taharah* must take place before one can be buried.

Those of us who attend to the body approach the deceased with a sense of holiness, and carry out our duties in awe, with reverence, respect, honor, and dignity.

The answer to the questions of "Why?" and "How?" is summed up well by this quote from Rochel U. Berman in the *Jewish Exponent* of Philadelphia.

"Finally when death comes . . . what remains is a sense of incompleteness, a need for spiritual closure. It is uplifting to know that at this venerable moment, I am able to perform the final act of love."

How did I get involved? One day over thirty years ago, my mother, of blessed memory, called me on the phone. It was neither a social call nor one inquiring about my or my children's well-being. It was a command call. Mother did not ask if you could do something; rather, it was "come and do it." The *it* was to assist her in a *taharah*, as she was short of help.

I knew that Mother was a member of the *Chevrah Kadisha*, for I knew how she dropped everything—from business obligations to personal appointments—whenever the funeral parlor or rabbi called her. However, I had no idea what it was that my mother actually did. I only knew that whenever a Jewish woman died, Mother was to the first to know, and off she went to the funeral parlor.

So when she called me, I too dropped everything, met her at the funeral parlor, and wondered (with trepidation) what it was I was expected to do.

Fortunately, Mother was a good teacher, and I was able to follow her instruction. So began a duty I faithfully fulfill to this day.

Now, looking back over those thirty years of performing *taharot*, doing them is more than following my mother's mandate. It is an unquestioned obligation to carry on so sacred a Jewish ritual—one that brings the life cycle to a close in a most dignified, compassionate, and reverential manner.

Several other dedicated workers also "drop everything" when the call for *taharah* is made. They are all religious, dedicated women, possessed of the strength and courage to proceed with this often-difficult mission. They are the women and men for whom the Jewish community is most grateful.

I also know, with great peace of mind, that when my time comes, I will be sent to my eternal abode with all the care, compassion, and blessings of those who will continue to uphold and perform the great mitzvah of *taharah*.

This article was first published in the *New Orleans Jewish News.*

Mildred L. Covert grew up, was educated, and married in New Orleans. She was always involved in Jewish life. Today four generations of her family have been involved in Chevrah Kadisha. Her grandmother used to do taharah on the kitchen table! Her mother and father were very successful business people, but her mother would leave her business to do taharah. This taught others the importance of this mitzvah. After the day Mildred was first called by her mother for help, she did this for more than forty years. Today a grandson does it as well. Mildred was an actor, and is a noted author of kosher cookbooks who has also published a book for children. She is celebrated enough that the Southern Food and Beverage Museum requested her papers for its archives. She is also a respected needlepoint artist. Now an octogenarian, Mildred no longer performs taharah.

Facing Impermanence

Rabbi Rachel Barenblat

The call came as I was nursing a mug of tea. The woman on the other end of the phone—I'll call her D—is a fellow congregant at my *shul.* We're both poets, both interested in *midrash,* so we've moved in similar circles for years, though I wouldn't call us close. She and her husband run our *Chevrah Kadisha.* They're always looking for volunteers, and at my first synagogue board meeting, Jeff urged us to consider joining them. He observed that in our tradition, this is the most sacred work one could do, a final act of respect toward someone who cannot conceivably repay it.

At the time, I was oddly tempted to volunteer. Though I'm comfortable with impermanence in theory, in practice it's difficult for me, and meeting death face-to-face seems like a way of accustoming myself to the koan: Do lives end? What does it mean to be embodied yet more than our bodies? What becomes of us when our bodies die? What does it mean to be holy in the face of finality and loss? These are some of the biggest questions I know, and serving on the *Chevrah*

Kadisha seemed like an opportunity to learn. But in the end, I didn't offer my assistance. I wasn't sure I was ready. I wasn't sure I had time. I let my excuses get in the way.

Until yesterday morning, when the phone rang. An elderly lady in our congregation had died, and D was looking for volunteers to help prepare her body, at 5:30 p.m., right after work. No time to equivocate, no time to postpone. Help was needed that day. I heard myself ask calmly how long the process usually takes; I reminded D that I'd never done this before, so I would need to be talked through it, and then I said I'd meet her at the funeral home. I hung up the phone not quite believing the conversation had been real. How on Earth would I get any work done, knowing that at the end of my workday, I was going to have my first encounter with death?

For a woman of thirty, I'm absurdly fortunate. I've lost grandparents, but I've never had to deal directly with death that came as a shock or seemed profoundly unfair. And until last fall, when my husband's grandmother passed away, I

had never actually seen a dead body. Jewish tradition teaches that the body of someone who has
died must be treated like the sacred vessel that it
has been, and prefuneral practices grow out of
the principle of *kavod hameit,* honoring the dead.
The *neshamah,* the soul, is believed to linger near
the body until interment, and our process of
taharah would prepare the body for burial and reassure the soul that its work here is done. Would
I be able to face the shell that had once housed a
human being?

When evening came, four volunteers were
present. All of us are on the synagogue's religion
committee, so we've worked together before. We
began in the funeral home parlor, perched on a
pair of sofas, reading psalms to center ourselves.
We prayed that we might see God reflected in
the face of the *meitah,* the person whose body we
were about to prepare, and also in each other's
faces as we joined in this work. "I'm glad you're
here," D said as we headed down the stairs to
the workroom, and I felt a wash of gladness too.

The steps of the process are simple. Wash the
hands (three times, as in any ritual hand-wash-
ing) and don gloves and aprons. Say a prayer asking the *meitah* to forgive you for any inadvertent
offenses or missteps committed during the
taharah. Wash the body lovingly with warm
cloths. De-glove. Ritually wash the hands again,
glove up again, and (since we have no *mikvah* to
immerse her in) wash the body with a constant
stream of poured water (nine *kavim,* or three
buckets full), repeating, *"tehorah hee"* ("She is

pure") together. Dry her. Dress her in hand-
stitched white linen: trousers, an undershirt, an
overshirt, and a tie around the waist. Sprinkle
sand from the Mount of Olives on her eyes, then
put on the facecloth and bonnet. Tie every set of
strings so that the loops form a letter *shin,* representing *Shaddai,* a name of God. Place her in a
simple pine box, on a white linen sheet, and
wrap the sheet over her before closing the box.

I felt unexpectedly calm throughout. It was
strange, seeing a body with no soul in it, stranger
still to wash her, an act that seemed impossibly intimate, but I was OK. I felt an outpouring of tenderness, occasionally giving in to the impulse to
stroke her hair or her arm, thinking, "It's OK, dear.
We're here. You're OK." Now and again, my mind
supplied me with moments of irreverence, as
when I glanced into the coffin (which must con-
tain nothing artificial and was lined with fine, curly
wood shavings) and thought of the straw nests in
which *etrogim* are shipped from Israel. The four of
us moved around the steel gurney like a team of
surgeons, handing each other washcloths and tow-
els, turning the body to wash and dry what we
couldn't easily reach. The woman's hands were
clenched but her feet were beautiful, and her
round belly. I wondered if she had borne children.

Jewish burial garments are the same for everyone, a reflection of our fundamental equality in
the eyes of God. The trousers are sewn shut at
the bottom so they concealed her feet; the
sleeves of the shirt were long enough to wrap
over the tips of her fingers. The sand we trickled

onto her eyelids was pale and golden, and somehow that was the moment when the irreversibility of the process hit me. It reminded me of the morning blessing praising God who removes sleep from our eyes and slumber from our eyelids. Some say the Jerusalem sand is used so that the first thing the deceased "sees" in the world to come will be the soil of the holy land, but to me it felt like we were providing the flipside to that morning blessing. In this embodied life, we thank God for opening our eyes; now we were marking the closing of her physical eyes. Maybe her *neshamah* no longer needed eyes to see.

We placed a linen cloth over her face, and tied the bonnet on, and then she was a bundled, white, human-shaped figure: no features, no distinguishing marks, only legs and arms, a torso and a head, a small, still, white figure. A little awkwardly, we lifted her and placed her atop the white sheet we had lain into the plain pine box, and wrapped the sheet over her, and then suddenly, out of the blue, I was shaking with silent tears. I leaned on the edge of the coffin of a woman I had never known, and understood what we had done for her, and wept and wept.

My three *chevrah* members clustered around me and hugged me. We maintained the silence we had held throughout (speaking only when we needed cues for lifting or moving her, and when we were taking turns pouring the unceasing stream of water that sufficed in place of *mikvah* immersion), and after a few minutes, I stood straight and peeled off my gloves and apron, and

we closed the box, and we hugged again, and then we walked away.

Tying the special *shin*-shaped knot was tricky. (Only one of the four of us had any facility with it). As we left the funeral home, one of my fellow *chevrah* members—a young great-grandmother but older than me by a long shot—turned to me and said, "When it's me on that table, don't worry about the knots!" We laughed then, all four of us, and even though my face was still wet, I felt good. Amazingly it was still light out when we left the funeral home (only an hour and a half had passed), and I felt dazed, a little giddy, as I headed toward my car. The evening was still and luminous, just barely warm enough for birdsong.

I can't say I came away understanding life and death. I can't say it was easy. But it seems right that we do this for one another. At Jewish funerals, mourners cast at least a symbolic handful of dirt onto the coffin: a final task we can perform for each other, a way of showing that we take care of our own, a way of reaching closure. Being a part of the *Chevrah Kadisha* is like that, just a lot more intense. We rely on each other, in the end.

Incarnation is a mystery. What we are, how we can be simultaneously holy-and-embodied (I thank God every morning for the miracle of my body) and holy-beyond-our-bodies (I thank God every morning for my *neshamah*, my soul, calling it pure in the exact same words the members of a *Chevrah Kadisha* will someday use to sanctify my body) is not something I can intellectually understand. But I know that I want to honor the whole journey, and that birth and death are points of contact with this great thing I cannot entirely grasp.

Death scares me. Not the fact that I will someday die but that those I love will die, that I will lose access to the people who shape my world. And I will. We all do. And that's OK; it's the rules of the game. Even now, people mourn the woman whose body I washed and dressed and blessed last night, and in performing this *mitzvah,* I connected myself with all of her mourners. With everyone doing those tasks all around the world. With the people who washed and shrouded the bodies of my ancestors, and the people who will sanctify the bodies of my children.

As a poet, I fear the lapse from sentiment into sentimentality, and I'm not sure how to talk about this without sliding into cliche. Clearly this had a strong impact on me; I dreamed last night that I was back in the basement room of the funeral home again today, preparing to do this duty again. (The dream depicted an impossible situation: a mixed-gender *chevrah* that included a young, male Buddhist monk in burgundy and saffron robes. Make of that what you will.) But here's what I know: There is nothing scary about touching a dead body. Doing so is human, and comforting, and sad.

It's good that D's call came out of the blue. I didn't have time to dream up excuses or to second-guess my assent. I was needed, and I stepped up, and the experience was deep enough that it kept me in the moment. And now I know that I can do this. It's strange and difficult, but it's also powerful. We're a small community; we celebrate a lot more *simchas* than we do losses. But I'm a part of my synagogue's *Chevrah Kadisha* now. It's like being in a volunteer fire department. I don't have to be there every week; it's not a regular part of my life. But next time the need arises, they can call on me. And now when I pray the words of the *amidah* which praise God who keeps faith with us beyond life and beyond death, they'll mean something new to me. I'm not sure I understand them, but that's OK.

This article was originally published at Velveteen Rabbi: http://velveteenrabbi.blogs.com/blog/2005/04/facing_imperman.html.

Rabbi Rachel Barenblat holds an MFA from Bennington College, was ordained by ALEPH: the Alliance for Jewish Renewal, and serves Congregation Beth Israel in western Massachusetts. Author of two poetry collections (70 Faces: Torah Poems, Phoenicia 2011, and Waiting to Unfold, Motherhood Poems, also published by Phoenicia, 2013), she has blogged as The Velveteen Rabbi since 2003, and has served on her community's Chevrah Kadisha since 2005. Find her online at velveteenrabbi.com. She lives in North Adams, Massachusetts.

Forever Changed

Ilene Z. Rubenstein

I am not a virgin anymore. Two summers ago, I participated in my first *taharah* (washing, dressing, and laying out the dead according to Jewish tradition). And just as when one loses that other virginity, I was transformed.

The day started like any other. It was sunny and bright, and I was about to get in the shower to get ready for work when the call came. As soon as I heard Rabbi Regina Sandler-Phillips' voice, I knew why the phone had rung. Even before she spoke, I was aware of an odd mixture of excited anticipation and dread. The women's *taharah* team of Congregation B'nai Jeshurun in Manhattan would be performing a *taharah* in a few hours. Its leaders had provided the initial *taharah* training for my *Chevrah Kadisha* (the Park Slope Jewish Center, Brooklyn's first "full service" non-Orthodox *Chevrah Kadisha*), and now they were inviting one or two members of our Park Slope women's team to participate along with them.

Prior care-giving experiences, study, and training had prepared me for this moment. I had taken part in the third North American *Chevrah*

Kadisha Conference at Columbia University, even though at the time I felt like somewhat of an imposter, never having personally participated in an actual *taharah*. I was more than ready to put theory into action, and yet I was also nervous. Was I really ready for this encounter with death? After all, it was only in the last year that I had dealt with enough of my "death issues" to be able to visit my father's grave for the first time. Had I resolved all my old issues as completely as I thought I had? Would I fall apart when actually confronted with my first *meitah* (deceased woman)? And there was also guilt: How could I feel excitement about this? But standing on the brink of a major step forward into new, uncharted life territory is exciting, and this was definitely new and uncharted—at least for me.

I quickly called my office to cancel my appointments and went upstairs. I was mindful of this being more than an ordinary shower, just as I was the morning I showered for my wedding. I was cleansing myself physically and spiritually to be ready to perform this *taharah* with the right kavanah (intention). As I planned what to wear, I recalled the usual advice to wear comfortable clothing since I would be there to work and not just to observe. Yet this did not feel right. I decided I needed an outfit that would be comfortable and allow unrestricted movement but also would express the respect this moment deserved, respect both for the meitah and for myself for taking this step. A long black skirt, new black top, and comfortable black sandals seemed appropriate. It felt right to wear something new for this new experience.

We are supposed to approach this work with reverence and humility, yet I couldn't help feeling proud of myself. I wanted to tell every other Jewish person waiting with me at the bus stop (easy to spot in my heavily Orthodox neighborhood!) that I was on my way to perform my first taharah. I whispered a "Shehecheyanu" (blessing for having reached this point) instead.

At the funeral home in Manhattan, Rabbi Regina introduced me to the rosh (team leader) and the other members of the B'nai Jeshurun taharah team. They were extremely supportive and welcoming, especially when they learned this was my "first time." We briefly discussed how the taharah would be conducted, and proceeded to the taharah area. I was told that I could leave and wait upstairs if the experience proved overwhelming. I knew I would not be judged if I did. We started putting on protective clothing and washing our hands in preparation for performing the taharah, and as we did, I felt feelings of ex-citement and dread and some small measure of panic rising inside me.

We wheeled the meitah from the refrigeration area to the taharah room. The bag containing her body was unzipped; I felt the dread rise to my throat. I glanced up and saw Rabbi Regina looking at me as if to say, "Are you OK? Do you need to leave?" Throughout the morning, as our eyes met, she silently asked the same questions. Her compassion and support sustained me, and I realized that I did not need or want to leave.

The moment I first glanced at "my" meitah, a rush of insights flooded me. Questions I had grappled with for years suddenly seemed to have clear answers. I saw that real death does not look like TV or movie death. Confronted by the cold, hard, unresponsive, colorless finality of death, I felt that I truly comprehended the awesome power of God for the first time because I understood the stark difference between life and death for the first time. I was able to grasp fully, for the first time, that only God has the power to create a living soul, and only God has the right to say when that life would end.

I suddenly realized that the thoughts of death that can creep into one's mind at times of deep despair bear little resemblance to the reality of death. The cosmeticized version of death we are so familiar with makes it easy to confuse death with a "time out" when coping no longer seems possible. In that piercing instant, I discovered new life-affirming boundaries. I appreciated more deeply than ever before the exquisite preciousness of life with all its joys and challenges, triumphs and pain. I understood, with clarity I had never known before, that death belongs to God. These boundaries filled me with peace, acceptance, and security.

My inclusion in the *taharah* was gentle and slow. First I joined in the recitation of the introductory prayers. We began to cleanse the *meitah*, and I was asked to clean her fingernails. I was struck by the coldness and rigidity of the body. But as we continued our ministrations, it seemed that her body became warmer and more pliant. Was it my imagination, or was she, even in death, responding to the warmth and love with which she was being prepared for her final resting place?

As the *taharah* proceeded, the deep beauty of this process struck me. In a quieter, less frenetic way, this woman was being cleaned, dressed, and readied to enter the next world with the same loving kindness that a newborn baby receives upon entering this one. As they worked, the team members sang *niggunim* (meditative melodies). Through them, in this sacred space, I heard the angels singing our *meitah* the ultimate lullabies. How could she not be comforted?

The *taharah* was concluded, and we gently laid the woman in her simple wooden coffin. We completed the liturgy and asked our *meitah* to forgive any disrespectful transgressions we may have inadvertently committed. We removed our gloves, washed our hands, discarded our hospital gowns, and prepared to reenter the world. Outside the *taharah* area, we spoke briefly about our experience together, and I was invited to ask any questions that I had before saying our goodbyes.

Walking out of the funeral home shortly after noon on that summer day, I was stunned to find that the sun was shining, as it had been when I arrived. Time and space had vanished in the *taharah* room, and it was startling to realize that outside, on Broadway, it was a normal day and life was moving along. But I was not ready to move *"mi kodesh lechol,"* from the holy back to the mundane. I needed to understand what I had just experienced. As supportive as the women on my team had been, I felt more comfortable asking Rabbi Regina my questions privately after they had left, and was grateful when she agreed to have lunch with me. This gave me the space to speak at greater length, and to slowly transition back to the everyday world. The *taharah* had literally been an awesome experience in that I was filled with awe: awe of God, the power of death, and a profound appreciation of the beauty of life. I felt uplifted and changed. I knew I would never be the same person again. How am I different? Like a girl who has become a woman: internally transformed and enriched, with a glow that may or may not have been showing. Since then, I have participated in several more *taharot*. Although my initial moments of fear have grown less intense, my sense of awe has not. I find that as the *taharah* itself washes away the smells and staleness of a body ravaged by age and disease, I start to see the person as the twenty-year-old who laughed and dreamed, who fell in love and was desired. The Song of Songs verses recited in the *taharah* liturgy put me in touch with the full beauty and richness of the life led by the person I am preparing, When she is dressed in her crisp, spotless *tachrichim,* I am reminded of the care with which she may have dressed for *Shabbat,* or to meet a lover. As we close the *aron* (coffin), and I say goodbye to my *meitah,* I no longer see someone aged and worn; I see a woman who in every way is the beautiful beloved described in the Song of Songs.

Have I gotten over my fear of death? Not entirely. But I have learned that I can face my fears and grow in spite of them. I have been blessed to have had a direct experience of God's presence once before in my life, when my mother was near death, but never before had I understood God's power quite so clearly. I feel clearer now about God's place in the world and about my own. This has made me feel stronger, more centered and connected to my community, especially those who partnered with me in *shmirah* (the traditional vigil over the dead) and *taharah,* and to Jews everywhere who have performed this holy work. I feel connected to a strong and beautiful heritage that has stretched back generations and generations and will reach forward to comfort and prepare me with love when my time comes.

This article was originally published in the spring/summer 2007 issue of *United Synagogue Review.*

Ilene Z. Rubenstein, LMSW, is a college adviser and counselor in Brooklyn, N.Y. She is a member of the Park Slope Jewish Center G'Mach Committee and Chevrah Kadisha. Other published articles by Ilene include "Mikvah of Possibility" in CJ: Voices of Conservative/Masorti Judaism *(Spring 2010) and "My Road to the Chevrah Kadisha" in* CJ: Voices of Conservative/Masorti Judaism *(Spring 2013).*

Sometimes participants can have a spiritual experience during the performance of taharah, as described in Gloria's story here. This is but one example of many possibilities.

Escorting the Dead

Gloria Itman Blum

It all began when the telephone rang to tell us that Pauline had passed away at the age of eighty-five. She had lived independently, and was the secretary of our Jewish congregation in Kailua-Kona on the Big Island of Hawaii. She was an observant Jew and took special pleasure in observing the sabbath as well as all the other Jewish holidays.

I hardly knew Pauline, but what I knew I liked. She was a *mensch* (a person having integrity). Even so, when we were told that she had passed on, I didn't feel particularly sad. She had lived a full, long life. Her family and community loved her. Now she was free of all the illness and discomfort she had endured. So it was OK with me that she was ready to move on. I continued to go about my day when the phone rang again. It was a rabbi from Honolulu asking my husband to ask me if I would participate, and would arrange for three other Jewish women to also take part, in Pauline's ritual bath before she was buried.

My initial response was, "Why me? Why not her women friends?" I phoned every woman on the island who I knew was her friend and about her age. Each had a reason she couldn't and/or wouldn't participate: "My heart couldn't take it. It would kill me"; "I'm still trying to get over my husband's death. I can't take any more."

I reassured each woman, "I understand. It's important for you to be true to yourself." I also understood that being older doesn't guarantee that one is spiritually mature enough to take on this ritual. It began to dawn on me that I was the one to lead the ritual bathing for Pauline.

One of my closest friends who knew and loved Pauline volunteered her services. I reluctantly declined her offer because I had been instructed that the women absolutely had to be Jewish. I was still alone on this mission. Then it hit me that I was going to know the intimacy of touching a dead naked body. What was I taking on? Was this for me?

I needed guidance from another woman. I phoned a wise friend to share my dilemma. A Mormon, she had performed similar bathing rituals for the deceased. She made it sound like a

neat thing to do for someone. I was feeling torn:
I didn't want to miss out on an honor of a lifetime, and I was squeamish about touching a
three-day-frozen, dead, naked, eighty-five-year-
old woman's body.

As Virginia spoke to me on the phone, I gazed
up and to the right and saw a most remarkable
presence: a vibrant yellow energy, almost
sparkling, which reminded me instantly of
Pauline's blonde hair. I sat there in a state of awe
when a voice spoke to me. I heard it with not my
ordinary hearing but a different kind of listening.
It was a very important message from Pauline.
She said, "I will be here for you as you are here
for me." I felt my soul quicken. I was touched to
the core. I bowed my head, honoring her presence. I heard myself speaking aloud, "How
sweet. How very sweet. Thank you. Of course,
I will be here for you." From that moment, my
mind was made up to lead the *Chevrah Kadisha*
as the "honored friend" of the dead.

I looked it up in a Jewish encyclopedia, which
said the *Chevrah Kadisha* is a "holy sisterhood"
for women who pass on, and a "holy brother-
hood" for men. "Escorting the dead," it said,
ranks among the basic humanitarian deeds. Burial society members who volunteer their services
are considered to be performing an "act of true
kindness" for which no reward or reciprocation
can be expected. In Judaism, burial of the dead
is deemed a religious commandment, a *mitzvah,*
one that takes precedence over even the study
of Torah.

The rabbi filled me in on the ritual bath procedure and again encouraged me to find two or
three more Jewish women to complete the desired team.

I phoned Ligia, a young architect and artist from
Romania whose father was a Holocaust survivor.
She immediately agreed to assist. The second
woman to accept was Carolyn, an unpretentious
and loving massage therapist originally from the
East Coast. Without hesitation, she said, "I'm
honored to be asked, and I would love to assist
you." The trio of Jewish women was in place.

In honor of Pauline's love for the sabbath, I
wanted the ritual to be completed on Friday afternoon before the sabbath began. The place
would be the hospital morgue, even though it
had no accommodations for our ritual. There was
not even a drain in the floor.

The keeper of the morgue initially told me that
two men from the hospital staff would help us
lift and stand Pauline up while we provided a
continuous flow of water over her head. I requested instead two women from the hospital
staff for the sake of modesty. Two gentile nurses
whom I knew graciously offered their services. I
wanted to do what was right according to correct
ritual for Pauline's sake, so I declined their offer
because they weren't Jewish.

The two nurses moved Pauline out of the
freezer onto a gurney. Her body was frozen with
indentations from the surface on which she had
been lying. Clearly, no life was left in this old
body. The three of us gasped as we saw blood

that had come out of her nostrils where there were still tubes connected. Ligia became faint. The nurses suggested we leave the morgue room for five minutes while they cleaned things up.

We steadied Ligia as she left the room, tears streaming down her face. She whispered, "It didn't hit me until I saw the blood."

We returned to the morgue and covered Pauline's corpse with a white sheet. It struck me funny that her right foot casually rested on her left ankle. I took Pauline's ice-cold right big toe and lifted the foot to place it alongside her left foot.

Five women encircled Pauline's body. Because the morgue was contaminated, each of us wore surgical suits, masks, booties, and gloves. We all looked the same dressed in the ritual garb of the operating room (or the high priestesses). As instructed by the rabbi, I said, "Pauline, we are doing this cleansing for your honor and ask your forgiveness if we don't do everything exactly as you would have wanted."

I closed my eyes and felt Pauline's presence, and spoke the following words: "Pauline, your lifetime here has been completed. Mazel tov! May the sabbath bride embrace your essence and guide you in peace and harmony. Return to your father. Feel his love for you and your love for him. You are free! Enjoy! *Shema Yisrael Adonai Eloheinu Adonai Echad*" (Hear O Israel, the Creator our God, the Creator is One).

Then with my eyes closed, I felt myself ascend up a shaft of life, of light, with the presence of Pauline to an open door filled with light. I went with her up to the doorway and lingered as Pauline passed through the light-filled door. How long did I linger? I was not in a world of time or space. Did I pierce the veil to eternal life? Something didn't feel right. I sensed something pulling at me. It was pulling me down. Suddenly it occurred to me that I was connected to something tugging at me, but what and why? In a flash I remembered. I had a body that I belonged in. I returned down the shaft of light to the density of my body, smelling the formaldehyde of the dreary morgue freezer room. I opened my eyes. I was stunned to see four tearful sets of eyes radiating love from behind their masks. These magnificent women were with me on this journey, and they knew in their hearts where I had been. We were one. We were all equally "Jewish" in that moment together.

Next we stood Pauline up, and with three buckets we poured a continuous flow of water over her head. Meanwhile, someone had started pounding on the morgue door yelling for entrance with another corpse on a gurney that needed refrigeration. I leaned against the door to keep it shut as the women laid Pauline back down and quickly toweled her entire body dry. As we put a special kosher cotton shroud on her, another fist started pounding on the door. A second corpse was now waiting to get in, and we felt the urgency to keep the ritual's momentum going. The door was being pushed open, so the nurses helped me keep it shut and lock it as everyone completed the process of fitting the little white bonnet onto Pauline's head and I tied the strings under her chin.

When we finished, I noticed that Pauline had again crossed her right foot over her left, which made me laugh, thank God. She was independent to the end.

The five of us joined hands with Pauline as Carolyn thanked Pauline and God for the honor of participating in this sacred ritual. We silently removed our surgical garb. We sensed that Pauline was comfortable and complete now.

Feeling numb afterward, Carolyn, Ligia, and I sat silently in Ligia's car, unable to move. Now, mission accomplished, I could allow myself to feel. My defenses dissolved as the impact of our experience hit me. Uncontrollable tears burst from my eyes, consoling and cleansing my soul.

We drove back to my house and drank slivovitz, listened to and sang, "My Yiddishe Momme," and shared a light, nourishing, quiet lunch together.

Several days later, we attended Pauline's funeral. The rabbi greeted me warmly, asking, "How did it go?" My response surprised me. "It was an honor for us, but I feel as though I lost my virginity!" A feeling of having lost something I didn't know I had . . . my innocence . . . forever gone. The rabbi understood immediately.

Gloria Itman Blum, M.A., created the curriculum guide, Feeling Good About Yourself *and the* Feeling Good Cards. *Voted Woman of Distinction by Soroptimist International of Kona, Hawaii, for outstanding contributions to her community, Gloria most enjoys producing community theater with meaningful Jewish themes, including* Fiddler on the Roof, I Never Saw Another Butterfly, The Diary of Anne Frank, *and her original musical* Abraham's Tent, *as well as singing in Kona's Traveling Jewish Wedding Band.*

With Woman, With Life

Tova Hinda Siegel

"Midwife" is a word in old German meaning "with woman." Historically, as well as today, it categorizes a specific profession in medicine. When I began my journey toward becoming a midwife, I was familiar with this definition. Most people, however, upon hearing the term "midwife" usually associate it as being "someone who, in taking care of the 'wife,' delivers her baby." There is little awareness about the many roles a midwife plays during the life cycle of a woman.

As a midwife, I have certainly attended many births, guiding women through the intensity of labor and delivering their babies. As the baby is born, I've lifted her to her mother's breast, and helped this new mother begin feeding her new baby for the first time. As a midwife, I also provide medical care, as well as emotional support, during pregnancy and after the birth, often looking after the newborn as well. Outside of pregnancy, I take care of women and girls of all ages, providing for their various health-care needs. In short, as a midwife, I have been "with woman" for the entirety of her life cycle.

In the last few years, however, I have become aware of a part of being "with woman" that was never covered in my medical training. I have become involved with performing *taharot* for Jewish women in Los Angeles. A *taharah* is the ritual protocol of preparation of a Jewish person for burial. It consists of a specific set of actions, delineated by Jewish tradition, which are performed by a group of women if the person is female and by men if the person is male. These groups are often volunteers and are known by the title *"Chevrah Kadisha."*

How, you may ask, can I compare *Chevrah Kadisha* work with that of providing women's health care? An interesting question—and yet I have experienced a reality that tells me this last act of caring for women is just a logical extension of the work I have been doing for so many years.

When a pregnant woman comes under my care, a sacred trust exists between us. Implicit in it is my saying, "I will be sensitive to you, to your needs. I will respect you and this new existence that you are creating. I will be there to help your transition from one state to another." Though not as dramatic or perhaps obvious, there is the same trust when a woman comes to me for gynecologic or general health care. I am promising that I will, to the best of my ability, be sensitive and caring, and attempt to fill her needs. I have always considered it a privilege, this work that I have been drawn to. I was blessed by the Lubavitcher Rebbe, Rabbi Menachem M. Schneerson, of blessed memory, when I began the process that led to my present career.

Several years ago, for reasons I could not begin to enumerate then, I began to feel myself drawn to the idea of becoming part of the *Chevrah Kadisha*. It took a while before I was able to begin the learning process and attend my first *taharah*. Many mortuaries have women on staff—wonderful, God-fearing, generous women who perform absolutely kosher *taharot*. By *hoshgachah pratit* (divine providence), I happened to ask a friend whom I knew had been doing *taharot* for several years to please call me the next time she went. "How about tonight?" she replied.

It somehow doesn't seem appropriate to use the term "excited" in reference to how I felt, knowing I was finally having the opportunity to begin this training. However, there was definitely an eager anticipation. Other emotions remain in my memory as well when I think of that night: nervousness, for one—how would I react? what if I did something wrong? I won't know what to do. As we were driving to the facility, I remembered that during my medical training, I had the same concerns with my first birth. This was fascinating to me. What was the similarity? Why did I feel the same way?

Our team also consisted of my friend, who had a lot of experience, and another woman whom I was meeting for the first time; she would be the leader, since she was the most experienced. We discussed the most likely scenario, and as I listened, most of my trepidation and anxiety melted away. I knew that I was in good hands and would be guided well.

We entered the room where we would be working and removed the sheets that had been covering the woman when she came from the hospital, at all times maintaining a respect for her modesty and dignity. I was reminded that when a woman is in labor, we likewise acknowledge the need for modesty and dignity. We behaved as we began the *taharah* in a manner of great sensitivity and caring, talking only when necessary to give instructions or lend clarity. The atmosphere in the room was one of deep consideration for this woman who was someone's wife, mother, daughter. Only actions necessary to accomplish the task were performed, always with minimal movement or disruption. There was a sense of depth, of spirituality and of connection, as we went through the ritual of the *taharah* and recited the *tefillot* (prayers). It was impossible to not be affected by this profound feeling.

When we finished our work, we asked "*mechilah*"—forgiveness—of this woman whom we had the privilege of assisting in her transition from one plane of existence to another. If we had done anything improper, some action not according to *halachah,* if we had caused any distress or humiliation, if in any way we were remiss, we asked that we be forgiven. At this last moment of being "with woman," I found that I was also asking that she please be an advocate for all Jews and beg *HaShem* to bring *Moshiach.*

We walked out into the night air, seeing a clear sky and feeling a deep quiet. I examined my feelings and realized that I felt as if I had been at a birth. There was the same silence, the same respect, the same depth of feeling, the same sense of privilege and the same knowledge that I had been given a gift of witnessing the transition of the soul. I knew with a certainty of understanding why I had been drawn to participating in this extraordinary *mitzvah.* Whatever it was that had propelled me to being "with woman" throughout their lives also drew me to being "with woman" as they leave this life. I felt that now I was truly a "midwife" in the fullest sense of the word.

Tova Hinda Siegel is a certified nurse midwife, providing health care to women of all ages in all stages of life over the last twenty-two years. She has delivered hundreds of babies, including many of her own grandchildren. Her interest in performing taharot rose as a logical extension of her profession caring for women. She started the first Lubavitcher Women's Chevrah Kadisha in Los Angeles, where she lives with her husband, Aryeh, and many children and grandchildren.

Caring for Those Who Have Died

Anna Rayne-Levi

In 2001, I began to study the practices of the *Chevrah Kadisha*. I took trainings in *taharah,* the Jewish ritual preparation of a person's body after death. I was fortunate to do several trainings in Albuquerque and Taos, and began to read about Jewish practices surrounding death.

I was particularly moved by the practice of keeping the deceased person company and staying near the body (the *meit* or *meitah* in Hebrew) while reciting psalms. I learned that in Judaism we "midwife" the soul by washing, praying, and preparing the deceased for its journey into the Mysterious Unknown. I call this Mysterious Unknown, God or *HaShem* or *Adonai* or *Shechinah*.

I cannot say why I was so moved to learn this ancient practice. I am a psychotherapist, and work with dying and grieving patients fairly regularly—mostly Catholic, Buddhist, or atheist. I have been called to the bedside of many dying patients and their families over the years. I assisted a close friend in her gentle passing in 1988 after a long battle with cancer.

Jeanette taught me a lot about living and dying with grace. She had been a hospice worker who studied with Ram Das, Elizabeth Kübler-Ross, and Stephen Levine. Her death transformed my life. I taught hospice workers in northern New Mexico, as a way to stay close to the dying process. It is impossible to put into words why I found death and dying so poignant. By staying close to death, I felt more alive and appreciative of the preciousness of life.

I was not called to actually perform a *taharah* until 2005. I had taken dozens of hours of training but had not had a chance to actually work with a deceased human body (rather than using life-size dummies or taking turns being the deceased during the trainings).

Then one morning in 2005, I got a call from the wife of an Orthodox rabbi, who also had not actually done a *taharah*. I in turn called a Reform Jew who had a lot of experience and another woman who had training but no experience, though she is very active in all the Jewish congregations in northern New Mexico. I was very nerv-

ous. I was terrified of making big mistakes. I
wanted to back out and offer some believable lie
as an excuse.

We all met at the funeral home in Santa Fe.
We prayed for guidance. We assigned the
woman with experience as our leader. We
walked into the refrigerated room where the
body of a woman in her nineties awaited us.
All my anxiety dissolved. I felt her presence, and
wanted only to do the very best job in preparing
her for her journey.

Then I stopped in my tracks and almost
stopped breathing. I saw the numbered tattoo on
her arm. I tried to imagine what horrors she had
experienced in the camps. How did she survive
and go on to such a long life? Who was she?
What were her dreams? Had she been able to
find peace? Was she a mother? A grandmother?
Was she funny? Was she kind? None of this mat-
tered, of course. Death is the great equalizer. But
I was very curious.

I stopped asking my mental questions and
went to work with our team of angels. We lovingly washed her. We recited the prayers in English and Hebrew. Some of us had tears in our
eyes. We asked for her forgiveness if we had
been clumsy. We gently dressed her in a simple
and beautiful shroud. We lifted her into a simple
pine casket. We placed small amounts of the
earth of Israel on her and pot shards over her
closed eyes. We closed the casket and prayed
some more. Then we lit a candle and placed it
on the casket.

When we quietly walked out of the room
(after removing our protective clothing and
gloves), a young man in an ill-fitting black suit
was standing there. He approached us with tears
in his eyes and thanked us. The woman was his
grandmother. (The work of the *Chevrah Kadisha*
is anonymous, and the presence of a family
member was a little awkward until we saw the
loving and grateful expression on his face.)

We met in a room to "debrief." It is important
to offer support to the members of the *Chevrah
Kadisha* after a *taharah*. Strong emotions can
arise. In our group, there were three "first-
timers." We promised to call our leader if we
needed to. We prayed some more. We talked
about the beauty of what we had all experienced.
We cried.

I went home, and gradually, the intensity of
the experience faded over the weeks. Then, in
July, I received a phone call from my sister. Our
eighty-three-year-old mother had suffered a heart
attack. I was able to speak to her and sing the
Italian lullaby she had sung to me every night as
a child; I was able to say "Grazie, Mamma." My
beautiful, feisty Mamma passed away within a
few hours. I was devastated.

In my mind and heart, I believe that I was
somehow being prepared for my own mother's
death during my first *taharah*. Losing my mother
was very hard, of course. I miss her every day.
But the beauty of the woman we midwifed after
her death helped me in ways that continue to
this day when I recite a psalm or help with a

taharah; the grateful look on her grandson's face will never leave me; the connection I felt with the other women in our *Chevrah Kadisha* continues to guide me.

Anna Rayne-Levy is a bilingual licensed psychotherapist in Santa Fe, New Mexico. She is a health-care and behavioral health-care consultant, and mother of a fifteen-year-old boy. She also teaches ways of integrating behavioral health with primary care to family practice medical residents at the University of New Mexico.

The Washer and the Washed: Bound in Sacred Duty

Lynn Greenhough

I am a member of a *Chevrah Kadisha* because I believe we are with God in life and in death; that we are with God in this life, *olam hazeh* and in the next, *olam haba.* While our very existence is testament to God's generous intention, it is hard for most of us to acknowledge such benevolence in the face of death. The mitzvah of *kavod hameit,* honoring the dead, grounds this intention by binding us to our community through shared ritual. In doing so, we not only bind our faith through that ritual but also recreate a stance of renewed optimism and trust.

As we begin the *rechitzah,* the physical washing, we acknowledge God's dwelling among us, even as the *meitah,* the dead person, has begun her journey from this world. We feel God's presence as we wash her hair, rinse it, and gently comb it free of knots. We hold her in transition between two worlds.

Judaism constantly challenges dualistic theol-ogy, emphasizing the profound connectedness of the spiritual with the material, the emotional with the physical. As we witness the changes in the body of the *meitah,* her limbs now leaden, so too do we sense her diminishing yet still sacred presence. Even as death brings *tumah* (impurity), this ritual of *taharah* brings about purification through poured water, prayer, and our collective attentiveness to death.

We proceed, first along her right side, and then the left, washing the body from head to toes. We enter into a scripted liturgy and ritual that acknowledges the sacredness of each life. These tangible rituals alert us to our sacred inter-dependence. Together, the dead and the living fuse in a cleansing ritual that is at once mundane and utterly holy.

The mitzvah of *taharah* purifies not only the person who has died but also us, the washers. As we pour water, as we gently wash fingers and toes, we too are wet with the *mayim chayim,* the living waters of cleansing. Into this room we bring the elements of life: candle, water, shards of clay to be placed over the eyes and mouth, and our own breath. We sense the holiness of our actions, the sacredness of each fingernail, stretch mark, and stitched incision. We approach each person as if he or she were a *Sefer Torah* inscribed by the Divine. Each time we touch death, we are renewed. These ritual gestures intimately bind us to each other.

Death demands. There is no argument, no procrastination. Death demands our presence, and death demands this ritual of physical and spiritual purification. Death demands that we re-member we are a tribe dedicated to *gemilut chasadim,* acts of lovingkindnesses—attending the dead but once. Each time I participate in a *taharah,* I am reminded yet again to show such kindnesses to the living, to not wait for their death to open my heart.

One of the texts that teach about our ritual relationship to the dead is called *Tractate Semachot.* In a telling textual conundrum, death and *simchah,* joyfulness, are blurred. Through these rituals, we encounter life and death, joy and grief. In facing death, we find the spark of holiness that binds us to each other and to God, and in the sharing of that spark, we know that what was shattered can be healed.

Lynn Greenhough has worked with the Chevrah Kadisha in Victoria, British Columbia, Canada, since 1996. This led to her 2000 master's thesis: We Do the Best We Can: Jewish Burial Societies in Small Communities in North America, *which looked at both the historical development of Jewish burial societies, and present-day membership and organizational structures. She is very grateful to her thesis supervisor, Rabbi Neil Gillman of the Jewish Theological Seminary. Lynn has presented at Kavod V'Nichum conferences on how to conduct a* taharah, *on the liturgy of* taharah, *and on the history of Jewish and Canadian cemeteries.*

Sometimes It's So Hard

Richard A. Light

There were just two of us today to prepare his lonely body.

At ten last night, the call came—*taharah* at 1 p.m. tomorrow.

A large man, just a boy really, he was barely twenty-five with beautiful long hair.

The rabbi was called while he was still hanging.

He had used a lamp cord in the garage. The wound on his neck was severe.

So gentle was his face—so soft his presence.

The tattoos seemed to express just the opposite.

We tended to his every need—he radiated when we were finished.

Inside he must have been so very special—yet somehow got so lost.

Ah, I am overwhelmed with sadness at the loss of such a beautiful son.

Just two of us to bathe him, dress him, honor him,

Yet I feel so honored to be here to help him—usher him on his way.

So healthy he looked—so not ready to die.

What pain can be so strong that a lamp cord on a rafter can be the answer?

So gentle.

So sad.

So unanswered!

Sometimes the impact of our actions is unknown to us yet can be significant. In this story, the circle becomes complete through unexpectedly related events.

Synchronicity

Laurie Dinerstein-Kurs

Early one morning, I received a phone call from a local Chabad rabbi. He told me that just a few minutes earlier, he had received a phone call from Israel—from a total stranger. The stranger had explained to the rabbi that her best friend lived in his neighborhood in New Jersey, and had died that morning. The woman implored the rabbi to get in touch with the *meitah*'s husband—who was not Jewish although the *meitah* was. Out of fear and concern for the *meitah*'s "final journey," the stranger from Israel had strongly requested that the rabbi ask the husband his burial plans.

The husband, having no clue as to what a "Jewish" funeral might consist of, had had the body of his beloved wife sent to a local non-Jewish funeral home for burial preparation. Coincidentally, the rabbi reached the husband in time to get his permission for the rabbi to arrange a Jewish burial. Coincidentally, the rabbi reached the funeral director before preparations had started. And the reason the rabbi called me early that morning was to see if I could arrange a *taharah* to take place in two hours. Coincidentally, I had not yet left for work and was home to receive his call. Coincidentally, the first three women I called were all available.

When we four women gathered to prepare for this special *taharah*, we learned that it was more unique than we had anticipated. Not all of us were prepared for what we found. This *meitah,* having donated much of her skin and many organs, was not exactly as intact as we may have preferred. Skin missing from her head and elsewhere made the amount of blood present not conducive to washing at all. Concave, open, and empty insides made moving her impossible without spilling volumes.

The *taharah* consisted mainly of our sensitive, caring decision to leave her alone. We removed her nail polish, flicked some water on her, recited all the appropriate prayers, put the *tachrichim* over her, closed the plastic body bag, and put her into the *aron*. We stepped back, said *mechilah,* and all went our separate ways.

A few weeks later, I happened to be visiting an

elderly aunt in New York, as my husband, Steve, and I do every few weeks. Our ritual for visiting includes leaving the house by 8:30, stopping for coffee, and being on the road by 9. We get to her apartment at 10:30, visit, schmooze, rehash old times, and leave about 1 in order to get home by 2:30 to walk the dog.

Coincidentally, this particular morning was her birthday. About 11:30, there was a knock at the door. Two little old ladies—one in a wheelchair assisted by an aide, and the other using a walker—had come to wish their friend a happy birthday. Both my husband and I gladly gave our seats to the aide and the lady with the walker. A few minutes later, another knock on the door, and two more friends appeared with birthday wishes. Between my aunt, her aide, four friends and another aide, and my hubby and me, room was tight. So we quietly departed and left the old friends to celebrate.

Coincidentally, leaving at this time—an hour early—turned out to be fortuitous because it gave me the chance to go into a local butcher shop to compare "our prices" with "theirs."

I looked at the cases in the back of the shop, saw nothing of interest, and turned to leave. On the counter I could see the screen of a computer that a female employee was using to search air flights.

Disappointment and sadness overwhelmed me, and I blurted out the fact that I was to have gone to Israel several weeks earlier but had turned in my tickets, as I refuse to go

through TSA requirements, and had forfeited my money. As I lamented my disappointment, the woman, who was from Israel, told me that while she was back there a few weeks earlier, she learned that her best friend, who lived in New Jersey, had died.

She said she had not had a peaceful moment since then because she was not sure her friend had been given a proper Jewish burial, since her friend's husband was not Jewish. When she learned of the death, she said, she went online to find a Chabad rabbi in her friend's neighborhood whom she called to explain the situation, and who assured her he would do his best to convince the husband to let the rabbi—a perfect stranger—intervene in the funeral plans. Since she was in Israel and her friend was in New Jersey, that was all she could do.

As I tried to console her, the similarity between what she was saying and the *taharah* I participated in several weeks before seemed too farfetched to be possible. There were too many coincidences. I asked her where in New Jersey her friend lived, who the rabbi was, and what day of the week she had called. Every answer made the hairs on my arm stand up.

I looked her straight in the eyes and was able to tell her that she could now be at peace—that I was the *roshah* of the *Chevrah Kadisha* that had cared for her friend, and I could assure her that her friend had been lovingly cared for and had a 100 percent kosher funeral.

She basically leaped over the counter and bear-hugged me—crying and laughing over the coincidence that I had happened into her store by chance, and that we happened to chat, and that now she knew for sure about her friend—and she could rest at night.

Steve, parked outside and watching through the window, could not understand why a woman would leap at me and bear-hug me without my seeming to be concerned.

While the women in my *chevrah* always feel a deep sense of the spiritual upon completing a *taharah,* we never know how it may affect family and friends.

Our devotion to performing *taharah* brought peace and comfort to someone in spiritual pain. As I stood there and realized the depth to which this woman had been affected, it was clear how important our work is for the living as well as the dead.

Coincidently, how great is that?

Laurie Dinerstein-Kurs is a mother of two and grandma of ten. Originally from Brooklyn, N.Y., she lives in East Windsor, New Jersey, and has been married almost forty-four years. After retiring from teaching, she became a clinical pastoral education chaplain. Laurie has been active in Chevrah Kadisha for close to thirty years. She serves as the roshah *for her community Chevrah Kadisha.*

Iris, Cleansed

Rebecca Jensen

Seven women were working around the body, which was lying on a chaise on the back patio, and the three oldest women were under the sheet that covered the body, cleaning the body off and washing her, and the buckets of water were filled by the men who were sitting with their backs to the women and the body, the buckets of water were kept filled and the pitchers were then filled from the buckets and the water was poured over the body, over and over and over, and the younger women held up the sheet keeping the sun from hitting the body, keeping the men from seeing the body, keeping the neighbors who might have gone outside at that moment from seeing the body, and the sheet was held up, sometimes getting in the way inadvertently, sometimes held to the side so they could see what was happening, and the older women had one long conversation among themselves which was the only conversation heard, telling each other to roll her one way and then roll her the other way, and the younger women read parts of the ceremony aloud, adding their voices to those of the older women, and a few poems were read, and a few prayers were read, and a few comments were made about the sheet, or the water, or the clothing that was used, and the older women dressed the body in the clothing that had been prepared the night before, the legs of the linen pants had been sewn together at the bottom, the shirt had been sewn together, too, linen from the pants had been used to make a head covering for the body which was part of the ceremony and which everyone there found funny because it appeared as though the head covering had ears, or horns, and everyone agreed the woman who had died would have enjoyed that since she had always insisted she was descended from Vikings who had raped and pillaged her Russian Jewish ancestors, and she would have loved the Norse look of her head covering, and finally the body had been washed and dried and dressed in the traditional linen clothing, and then the younger women dropped the sheet over the woman on the chaise to cover her one last time, and then the young men got up from their chairs and picked up the chaise to get it out of the sun and they put it on top of the hot tub under the redwood trees since that was the only shade easily accessible, and I thought the woman who had died would have liked that, too, to be carried by her grandsons and great-grandson like the prima ballerina she was when she was alive being carried offstage, and the women hugged each other and cried and talked about how amazing this experience had been and how happy they were that they had done it, and how lucky they all were that the woman had died there, in her grand-daughter's home, surrounded by so many members of her family so that she could be cared for, and that this ceremony could be performed by members of the family and not strangers, and the funeral home was called and they came within the hour and they took the woman off the hot tub and apologized to the family for having to strap her to their gurney so tightly, and the women and the men all came outside to say their last goodbyes, and then Iris was taken away, to be cremated, after three days ending two weeks of intense, emotional caregiving by her family.

Rebecca Jensen was privileged to participate in the taharah *for her grandmother, Iris, in June of 2001. She is an artist and writer living in Oakland, California, with her wife and their cat.*

My Traditional Jewish Burial Ritual Story

Joyce Kendall Friedman

I waited a year after my mother (may she rest in peace) passed away before I was able to think about doing for others what the *Chevrah Kadisha* had done for her. I read the manual I was given that Rabbi Stuart Kelman had written. My friend, Helene, suggested that I watch the first time and read the prayers in English as she read them in Hebrew. Having worked in hospitals and nursing homes, I was not a stranger to illness and death, but this was not medical. This was spiritual and kind and gentle. It was easier for me than I had expected; it was even a relief. I saw and felt what these women had done for my mother. I was so grateful. I was comforted and felt that my mother must have felt comforted too. These women, these *Chevrah Kadisha* members, were the embodiment of the God's feminine aspects: compassion, kindness, nurturing.

Our *meitah* was cold. We covered her body and face modestly. We called her by her Hebrew name as we apologized for any unintended disrespect. We noted that we were going to do the "best we could." We quietly prepared the implements, assigned duties, and began checking her for bandages, medical devices, and nail polish, areas that needed special cleansing. We said the prayers in the manual and were comforted by the excerpts from the Song of Songs, describing her beauty. We were reminded not to pass items over her, as her *neshamah* (soul) hovered just above her. We tried to remember not to stand at her head as the *Shechinah* (God's presence) hovered there. Occasionally we spoke to her in comforting tones, as we had read that the sense of hearing was the last to go. We knew she was listening. We reminded her that we intended only respect and kindness.

We cleaned her, combed her hair, and then ritually purified her with the three buckets of continuous flowing water and more prayer. We dressed her as the high priest in the Temple was dressed, with pure white garments. We lifted her into the plain pine box and wrapped her in a white cloth after sprinkling her with earth from Israel's Mount of Olives. We faced her feet toward the door, beginning her journey to Paradise (*Gan Eden*). Again, we addressed her and asked for her forgiveness. The other women had done this many times before and still were moved and impressed with the significance of the moment.

I felt quietness envelop me, as I had been privileged to participate in a transition from one level of existence to the next. What an honor it was to be there with her. I felt reassured that this had been done for my mother and one day would be done for me. In a way, it was as if I was privileged to be a voyeur, sneaking a glimpse into the next world. I came away reassured.

Joyce Kendall Friedman, Ph.D., lives in Oklahoma City. She is a licensed clinical psychologist specializing in pain and stress management, and a recognized expert legal witness specializing in the psychological aftermath of traumatic injury, particularly aircraft accidents. She also has been involved in all aspects of Chevrah Kadisha work, and links chaplaincy work with Jewish death practices in beautiful ways.

Under a Tree

Zoe Ariana Van Raan

She killed herself under a tree in the wilderness, with the intention of not being found until well after the process of bodily death was complete. Days later, I stood in front of her casket. In the final few months of her life, the woman—I'll call her "J"—had sought out a Jewish community and declared immense gratitude for having found some solace from her depression through attending sporadic services. Surrounded by a very open, welcoming, and supportive congregation, she spoke from a place of vulnerability that was otherwise masked by her reserved demeanor, rumpled jeans, and sandals. She spoke about the deep depression within which she found herself. Her illness, the specifics unknown to the congregants, deprived her of sleep, and therefore of peace of mind.

Her loneliness was apparent, so members of the congregation banded together and reached out to offer friendship through homemade food, companionship, and attentive, compassionate ears. But this attention seemed to fade in and out as their energy was diverted by their own busy lives. Still, the woman knew that if she reached out, someone would surely be there with her. In the end, those who befriended her knew that they did the best they could, enabling her to feel love before the inevitable happened.

Our *chevrah,* accustomed to two or three deaths per year, received the *mitzvah* of four deaths within three days: In addition to the depressed woman, there was a young mother whose teen-age son had tied the last knot and covered his mother's face with lace after her *taharah.* I guided her friends and family through the processes and procedures from the evening she died in her home through the time of the burial. Another was an elderly man who did not have friends or family, only a caretaker of Catholic and Arab descent. The tireless, almost-desperate effort she put into assuring that his wishes would be fulfilled and he would have a traditional Jewish burial was awe-inspiring, and touched us deeply. I stayed on the phone with the caretaker late into the night as she mourned loudly, beseeching God to take him while searching through his paperwork to find his Hebrew name and any semblance of documented history that could be used for a proper eulogy. The final death was a beloved member of the community who died after a long, full life.

I stood in front of J's casket, alone, depleted after an entire week of emotional interfacing with the families and logistical juggling with the members of our *chevrah* and the funeral home, as well as being the sole organizer of seamless *shmirah* and three *taharot*. Because of the extent of decomposition and other natural consequences of lying in the wilderness for days, as well as having undergone an autopsy, we could not perform a *taharah* or even open the body bag for the woman who had killed herself in the wilderness. Thinking I was fulfilling an important closure, yet feeling that it was a mere formality, I began to recite the *Chamol*[8] prayer. Since she was not receiving a *taharah*, it was the only prayer from our manual that I could recite. I then read it in English, and was astounded by the relevance of the words to her particular life.

Consequently, for the first time, I actually connected the liturgy with the *meitah*. At the same moment as I was feeling that connection, I felt and saw the last part of her soul rise up. It was in the form of a jagged, triangular shape. I encouraged the soul to move on, and it did. In contrast with my previous experiences of slight distress over not feeling the "spiritual" aspect that so many other people seem to feel during the ritual, I felt it now: true closure for her soul, and my capacity to guide it toward God and the next part of her journey.

Zoe Ariana Van Raan is a roshah *within the women's team of the Chevrah Kadisha of Northern New Mexico. She holds a degree in political science, is a mother, Jewish educator, and hospice volunteer, and works for the New Mexico Suicide Intervention Project. She is aspiring to become a rabbi. Zoe lives in Santa Fe, New Mexico, with her wife and daughter.*

It Came That Day of Its Own Accord

Richard A. Light

Spontaneously it came—

Effortlessly flowing over and through me.

At first it was just a feeling—a faint hint of an essence.

Slowly it grew into a hum.

Unknown, unrecognized, the tune supported me.

It peeled the layers within me, opening me to the blessing of the day.

Silently he lay there.

Joyfully I worked. The tune carrying my joy—expanding me, helping me be.

Effortlessly he and I created the tune—and soon I was not separate from it.

Still I could not name the tune.

And he was so silently there, yet so present.

Other team members resonated with it, flowed with its guidance.

We finished our work, but the tune was not finished with us.

Finally, as we departed it came to me.

What it was that I was, that was singing me.

Shehecheyanu!

Thank you for this day!

Setting Aside the Super Bowl, Just Once, for a Holy Act

Rabbi Chaim Steinmetz

Most of life is a balancing act. Many different obligations and interests are competing for our attention, and we try to balance them all. We do our best, planning, prioritizing, and managing our time. Sometimes, we realize what our true priorities are when our plans fall apart.

When I lived in New York, I was a member of a *Chevrah Kadisha.* Four years ago, on Super Bowl Sunday, I was planning to spend the evening relaxing and watching the game. It had been a difficult week, and I needed a break. That afternoon Nina, a *Chevrah Kadisha* member, called. She desperately needed a volunteer for a *taharah,* and wasn't taking no for an answer. Well, there are only so many excuses I could give before finally saying yes. I reluctantly agreed, realizing I would have to miss a full hour of the Super Bowl. I joined the other volunteers in a side room at Riverside Memorial Chapel, preparing a fellow Jew for his final journey.

Walking home from the *taharah,* I thought about how odd it was to go from the Super Bowl to a *taharah,* and how different these two events are. The Super Bowl is a celebration of human power and might. Winning is everything. The members of the winning team, after endless training in the weight room and on the practice field, are now declared champions. The losers are forgotten. As former Oakland Raiders Coach John Madden once said: "The only yardstick for success our society has is being a champion. No one remembers anything else."

The perspective of a *taharah* is very different.

Rabbi Moshe Sofer explains that the main purpose of the *taharah* is to preserve the dignity of the deceased, because each person is made in the image of God. During a *taharah,* the dead body is meticulously cleaned, with great care taken not to move the body in a demeaning manner. Afterward, it is placed in a *mikvah,* a ritual bath, to achieve a spiritual purity and is dressed in a modest white shroud. The *taharah* is a final act of respect given by the community to a fellow Jew, because even the lifeless body of a dead person deserves our respect.

The Super Bowl and a *taharah* offer two very different views of power. At the Super Bowl, greatness is only for the powerful and the strong; the losers are relegated to the dustbin of history. At a *taharah*, there are no losers. All human beings, even the weak and unknown, are treated with great respect because they are in God's image.

As I got home that night, I sat down to watch the end of the Super Bowl. My plans for the day had changed but so had my priorities. I can't remember anything about that Super Bowl, but I will always remember that *taharah*.

Chaim Steinmetz is a rabbi, writer, and activist. He has been a congregational rabbi for nearly two decades, and has served as the spiritual leader of the Tifereth Beth David Jerusalem Synagogue in Montreal since September 1996. Before that, he served congregations in Mount Vernon, New York, and Jersey City, New Jersey. He has been involved in many community organizations, and is a member of the board and a past vice president of the Federation-CJA of Montreal. He has officiated at hundreds of funerals and many more joyous life-cycle events.

מוות בתמיכה הדדית

Mutually Supportive Death

David Zinner, one of today's foremost experts on Jewish death practices, writes:

> Judaism is about life: the opportunity to do good, to create, to make the world a better place. Unlike many other religions, the Jewish focus is not on the afterlife; it is on *olam hazeh,* on the here and now. When we concentrate on death, it is because it is a part of life, although a part that is often ignored or denied. Mortality is what we all have in common. How we deal with death, our attitudes, our practices, our institutions, are a reflection of our approach to life.[9]

Where Did All This Come From?[10]

In Judaism, death is a communal matter. Although today's model of who in the community does what job was not always the case, the role of the community in death rituals has been with us since biblical days. The tradition of a dedicated burial site starts with Abraham, who bought a piece of land specifically to bury Sarah and serve

for his family as a place of burial. The custom of the community mourning for thirty days is clearly described as the people mourned the deaths of Aaron (Numbers 20:24–29), Miriam (Numbers 20:1), and Moses (Deuteronomy 34:1–8). What is not in the *Tanach* (Torah, Writings, and Prophets) is the establishment or discussion of the *Chevrah Kadisha,* nor any organization to arrange, handle, and be responsible for taking care of the dead. Perhaps because it was obvious, no one ever wrote it down. There exist only a few written indications.

In writings after 1000 C.E., we find that a formal element of the community was in place to handle the dead. During the period of the *Rishonim,* the earliest post-Talmudic rabbis (1040–1350 C.E.), four major developments happened simultaneously but independently that significantly impacted the history of *Chevrot Kadisha* development. These are:

- The establishment of communal Jewish cemeteries outside of Israel;
- The first *responsa* mentioning the *Chevrah Kadisha;*

- Additional written commentaries on the death, burial, and mourning portions of the Talmud;
- Further compilations of customs and laws related to illness, death, and mourning.

Regarding the latter, Zinner clarifies the importance of these compilations:

> Torat ha-Adam (Law of Mankind) was written by Nahmanides Ramban (1194–1270). It represents a major step in the evolution of *Chevrah Kadisha* literature because it is the first post-Talmudic comprehensive collection of customs and laws specifically focused on the continuum of illness, death, and mourning. Its thirty-six chapters cover every aspect of the end of life from the onset of serious illness to what is prohibited and permitted and what is a *mitzvah* as regards the sick and dying. This is followed by a comprehensive guide to the laws of mourning. The pattern of sickness, death, burial, and mourning was used as a template for many works on the subject including the *Tur* by Jacob ben Asher (1269–1340), the *Shulchan Aruch* by Joseph Karo (1488–1575), and to this day in *The Jewish Way in Death and Mourning* by Rabbi Maurice Lamm.[11]

By the late 1300s, the evolution of the full-fledged *Chevrah Kadisha* began in earnest because of the emigration of Spanish Jews and the rise of Lurianic Kabbalists. As the communities of exiled Jews migrated, the proliferation of burial societies followed them. The central role of the *chevrah* in each community helped support its health, no matter where it moved. In the early 1600s and again in the early 1700s, we begin to see specific publications directed to the *Chevrah Kadisha*. One of the most noteworthy is the publication in 1626 of *Ma'avar Yabbok* by Aaron Berechiah ben Moses ben Nechemiah of Modena, which was considered the most comprehensive compilation at that time of Jewish laws, prayers, and customs related to sickness, dying, burial, and mourning. This was followed in 1703 by the publication of *Sefer Hachayim* by Simeon Frankfurter, and circa 1750 by *Sefer Sha'ar Shimon* by Moses Frankfurter. These set the stage for how to visit the sick, tend to a dying person, and bury our dead.

In the late 1800s, as Jews immigrated to North America, they brought with them their European customs of *Chevrot Kadisha*. However, the New World had other plans. As the establishment of funeral homes and the professional funeral director evolved here, those who wanted to assimilate and escape from their pasts were eager to let others deal with death. Again, Zinner explains:

> Despite the Jewish community's strong attachment to the *Chevrah Kadisha* tradition, the transition from simplicity to ostentation, from the *Chevrah Kadisha* to the professional funeral director, was so

rapid that in 1915, Sholom Aleichem wrote a satirical story [about this ostentatiousness] called *Beryl Isaac and the Wonders of America*.

This trend toward ostentation was intertwined with the development of a uniquely American institution: the for-profit funeral home. The tensions, struggles, and strained relationships among funeral homes serving Jews, the Jewish religious establishment, and the *Chevrah Kadisha* were set within a uniquely North American cultural and capitalist environment. Traditional Jewish funeral and burial practice was at the center of a tug-of-war, pulled, pushed, stretched, and distorted by those with an economic stake in the outcome.[12]

Despite this, Jewish communities have continued to create, support, and use *Chevrot Kadisha* to handle their dead. Since the 1960s, interest has gradually increased in a return to traditional Jewish practices. As a result, there is a thriving North American movement today to promote, teach, and support these practices and move away from the ostentatious and economically driven death model of American society.

Mutual Support

Jewish death practices are designed to support individuals through community-organized rituals and events tied to the stages of death themselves.

These practices benefit not only those who are directly involved but those in the community who are in support roles as well. For example, when there is a death, the entire community takes part. Several "players" are directly involved—the deceased, the family, and those who prepare the deceased for burial (the *chevrah*)—but there also are players who are not directly involved—those who prepare the meal of consolation for the mourners, those who fill in the grave, those who show up to provide a *minyan* so *Kaddish* can be said, and those who visit the mourners at their home. Each of these provides service for the community, and each may receive benefit of some kind, although the *Chevrah Kadisha* members receive only the good feeling that comes from helping someone who cannot thank you, and the nontrivial experience of midwifing a soul from this world to the next.

In return, this death cements the community as a family. It shows each member that "we care" about each other, and we will be there when someone needs support. It brings death out of the closet, revealing that which our society denies, and shows everyone how to celebrate this life-cycle event. And it reminds us all to live each moment wisely since our days are numbered.

The *Chevrah Kadisha* team members are blessed with the unique opportunity to strengthen and deepen this mutually beneficial arrangement within the community. They have the knowledge and tools to prepare the dead for burial through *taharah*, and are often involved in arranging *shmirah* and burial, but they have the additional responsibility to help educate the community about the beauty and simplicity of Jewish death and burial rituals. This role can take many direct public education shapes: community talks, workshops, panels of speakers, roundtable discussions, community meetings, and *divrei Torah.*

The scope of activities of the local *Chevrah Kadisha* can vary from community to community. In some, their only focus is *taharah.* Other groups can encompass a broad continuum of activities such as visiting the sick; guiding the family through the death process, burial, and mourning; preparing the body for burial (*taharah*); arranging *shmirah;* arranging the burial; filling in the grave; creating the meal of consolation; supporting the *minyan* at the home of the mourners; offering to do chores for the mourners during *shiva;* and doing public education programs. All of the *chevrah* prac-

tices are based on local *minhag,* the customs that have evolved over time for each community. Most *chevrot* today focus only on *taharah* and possibly *shmirah,* leaving the rest of this large continuum to other community resources.

These can be significant, and contribute extensively to the health of the community. Hospice groups, chaplains, and caring committees work tirelessly to help families cope when death comes. Music thanatologists help to ease the process of dying and comfort families. Regular synagogue services support the community's spiritual needs, and provide the basis for mourners to say *Kaddish.* Rabbis are always available for guidance when death looms. And lastly, local funeral homes and Jewish cemeteries also are part of the equation, providing an important part of the foundation that supports the health of the community.

To Enter the Liminal Space

To understand the power of Jewish burial practices, one must understand, at least to a limited extent, the amazing transformative nature of *taharah*. We come close to the veil, the boundary between death and life, as we enter into an intimate relationship with those who are in transition between this world and the next. The personal stories we have explored give a hint of what it feels like to enter this "liminal space." Let's now take a look now at the structure of this powerful ritual, the beauty of its nature and flow, and the essence of its words.

An Overview of Taharah Ritual Procedures

The *taharah* ritual is usually composed of the following major parts, each of which has specific readings that accompany the ritual actions:

1. Briefing;
2. Preparations and setting intentions;
3. Washing the deceased physically (*rechitzah*);
4. Spiritual purification (*taharah*);
5. Dressing the deceased in special clothes (*halbashah*);
6. Preparing the deceased for transport, usually in a casket (*halanah*);
7. Cleaning up;
8. Debriefing.

In the first part of the ritual, the team is briefed on how the death occurred, the Hebrew and English names of the deceased if known, and any special circumstances that need to be taken into account, and tasks are assigned to the team members. A group prayer usually follows in which the *taharah* team asks God to protect them and help them to do their work and see the holiness of the Divine in the deceased and in each other as they do their tasks.

Then the team enters the preparation room in silence. The members don personal protective clothing and begin the first task, washing the body. Any clothes on the body are removed, along with any medical devices that can be removed safely, and the body is covered with a sheet. This is followed by a gentle bathing: cleaning fingernails, toenails, combing hair, washing all parts of the deceased's body carefully and thoroughly, and then rinsing the body, much like washing a baby. All of this is accomplished while the deceased is covered; a *chevrah* team member lifts up a corner of the sheet and washes that area, then replaces the corner of the sheet. At all times, the modesty and dignity of the deceased is preserved. The body is prepared with the same kind of care one might use when preparing for one's wedding. When the washing is completed, a new, clean, dry sheet is placed over the deceased.

The spiritual purification section, the *taharah* itself, is usually accomplished either by immersing the body in a *mikvah* (special spiritual bath), or by pouring nine *kavim* (twenty-four quarts) of clean water over the body in a continuous flow, simulating the action of a running stream. When the purification is complete, both the table and the body are dried completely, and the deceased is covered with another clean, dry sheet. In Judaism, *mayim chayim,* living waters, play a central role in our history and traditions. Water is truly a primal transformative element.

Now the deceased is dressed to meet his or her Maker in clothes that represent those worn by the high priest, the *kohen gadol,* for we are all as holy in death as the holiest of our people. These clothes or shrouds, called *tachrichim,* generally include pants with the feet sewn shut, a shirt, a jacket, a head cover, and in some cases additions for women that include a veil and an apron. Closures at the neck and waist and around the legs are tied with knots in a special way that represents Hebrew letters for one of the names of God. The specifics vary from community to community, but usually knots for all areas but the waist include one or two Hebrew letters, while the *gartel,* or waist belt, is tied in an even more special way to include *shin, dalet,* and *yud,* to encode a full name of God into the clothing. The clothes are simple, white, hand-sewn linen or cotton muslin. All Jews are buried the same: rich, poor, famous, or unknown. We are all equal in death.

Once dressed, the deceased is placed into the waiting casket in which a diamond-shaped *sovev,* or burial sheet, is placed diagonally, so the deceased can be wrapped up like a swaddled baby, with the feet covered first, then the right side, then the left side, and lastly, the head. Before this, men and some women are wrapped in a prayer shawl (*tallit* with one or more *tzitzit* removed). Pottery shards are usually placed over the mouth and/or eyes, and earth from the holy land of Israel is often sprinkled on the heart, genitals, and face, and throughout the casket. The *sovev* is wrapped around the deceased, and often at this point, the deceased radiates! It's quite amazing. The lid is secured in place, and the *chevrah* members surround the casket to ask for forgiveness for any act they might have done that did not honor the dignity, modesty, and respect of the deceased.

The deceased is then placed outside the preparation room with a lit candle, and possibly a *shomer* to accompany the casket, while the team cleans up the preparation room. Finally, the *taharah* team assembles in a convenient place other than the preparation room to debrief. The emotional health of the team is paramount, so the day's ritual events are discussed along with any trauma or confusion that occurred. If necessary, arrangements are made to follow up on any issues that came up during the ritual, either emotionally within the team or practically related to supplies or facilities, etc.

אֲשֶׁר בַּיהֹוָה אֶת

יַעְטֵנִי כֶּחָתָן יְכַהֵ

וְכַגַנָּה זֵרוּעֶיהָ תַצְמִי

גּוֹיִם לְמַעַן צִיּוֹן

The Power of Words—The Taharah *Liturgy*

What should one say to help a soul move from this realm of existence to another? How does one create a catalytic ritual that works in the practical sense of moving the soul between worlds but also is comforting to the soul as it faces the loss of its body and the unknown future ahead? Luckily for us, we have inherited a flow of readings that do both of these things very well.

Rabbi Stuart Kelman, a founder of the Gamliel Institute, a center for study, training, and advocacy concerning Jewish death-related practices, and a well-known liturgy scholar, notes that there are five concepts behind the *taharah* liturgy,[13] namely:

- The interplay between *tahor* and *tamei* in the preparation room, which do not necessarily only mean pure and impure (as they are usually translated). Rather, they are the extremes of unholy and holy states of being, where, as Kelman says, "A human corpse embodies the most extreme version of the state of being *tamei*, and the state of being *tahor* was a requirement for participation in all of the most important religious rituals in the ancient temple."[14]

- Using the traditional *tachrichim* (burial clothes) as a means for the deceased to get close to God, much as the *kohen gadol* (the high priest in the days of the temple) got close to God partly through the clothing (specified in Leviticus 16:4) that he was to wear when he approached the inner sanctum. "His special clothes were one of the factors that changed the nature of this interaction between human and the Divine, elevating it from a mere encounter to a unique and powerful moment."[15] We dress the dead essentially in clothes identical to those specified for the *kohen gadol* to express our hope that the deceased will also attain closeness to God.

- The concept of how a new head priest could become pure to do his job in the days before the destruction of the temple. Zechariah (520 BCE) tells us that the angels would remove his clothes and redress him in the priestly garb. One of the angels said that if Joshua performs his priestly duties properly, he would be permitted to move around in heaven as well as here on Earth as the *kohen gadol.* In death, the deceased is much like this, still on Earth but moving into heaven.

- The presence of the *neshamah,* or soul, living on after death: Everything in the *taharah* liturgy assumes this to be true, and that the soul is present in the preparation room. Our task is to assist the *neshamah* on its potentially confusing and possibly dangerous journey, just as we assist the body on its more-mundane journey.

- The Song of Songs (*Shir HaShirim*) is used to establish a new relationship between God and the deceased. The verses can be interpreted in two ways: between God and the Jewish people, or between a man and woman in love. In this case, it is between the newly deceased soul and God. The soul is about to be reunited with God, like a groom with his bride.

The readings of the *taharah* liturgy included in most modern *taharah* manuals are not prayers per se but quotes from the *Tanach* or *Talmud,* or related documents that apply specifically to the sections of the *taharah.* They include quotes from Rabbi Akiva and readings from the *Song of Songs* and Zechariah, among others. A learned Gamliel student, Deborah Brown, described taharah liturgy during a recent Gamliel Institute class discussion:

> For a few years before I came to Judaism, I attended silent Quaker meetings. The silence was such a beautiful space into which one could breathe oneself and become reacquainted with the breathing. A lot of people just can't imagine why anyone would want to do that, nor do they get why it is important to do it with other people rather than just alone. I think a *taharah* is a sort of group silence, a space removed from the busy lives we lead, where we lift up the deceased with our silence. Yes, I know there is a liturgy, but it is really a silence that we offer, a space for the soul to move into and then away from the body. The liturgy just points to something that we don't really understand. It vocalizes our longings.

When analyzing *taharah* liturgy, Kelman reminds us to consider these things:

- Who is in the *taharah* room?
- What does each entity need to say to or on behalf of the other parties?
- What questions do the elements of the liturgy answer? Why were they included?

In general, three main entities along with two groups of heavenly creatures are involved in a *taharah*: the deceased, the *chevrah* team, and God, along with the angels and demons (or demonic and/or dangerous forces). All of these are referenced in the liturgy. The interactions among them, which have been discussed for centuries, and the questions answered by the liturgy are what make the *taharah* work. To give an idea of what the liturgy is composed of, here are some excerpts:

As the *chevrah* team begins the ritual, the following is said for a deceased male. (The female version is similar with different pronouns.)

> Ruler of the Universe! Have compassion for _____, the son of _____, this deceased, for he is a descendant of Abraham, Isaac, Jacob, Sarah, Rebecca, Rachel, and Leah, your servants. May his soul and spirit rest with the righteous, for you revive the dead and bring death to the living. Praised are you who pardons and forgives the sins and trespasses of the dead and your people, Israel, upon petition. Therefore, may it be your will, Adonai, our God and God of our ancestors, to bring a circle of angels of mercy before the deceased, for he is your servant and son of your maidservant. And you, Adonai, our God and God of our ancestors, who is concerned with the poor, save him from all misery and from a day of evil and from banishment. Blessed are you who makes peace in the heights for your servants and for those who revere your name. . . .

As we take the clothes off the deceased:

> And he (the angel of God) raised his voice and spoke to those who were standing before him, saying, "Remove the soiled garments from him (the high priest)." And he said to him, "Behold, I have removed your iniquity from you, and I will clothe you in fine garments." (Zechariah 3:4–5)

As we wash a deceased male (a similar but different reading is used for females):

> His head is burnished gold, the mane of his hair black as the raven.
> His eyes like doves by the rivers of milk and plenty.
> His cheeks a bed of spices, a treasure of precious scents, his lips red lilies wet with myrrh.
> His arm a golden scepter with gems of topaz,
> His loins the ivory thrones inlaid with sapphire,
> His thighs like marble pillars on pedestals of gold.
> Tall as Mount Lebanon, a man like a cedar!
> His mouth is sweet wine, he is all delight.
> This is my beloved and this is my friend, O daughters of Jerusalem. (*Song of Songs* 5:11–16)

Before the spiritual cleansing:

Rabbi Akiva said, "You are fortunate, Israel. Before whom do you purify yourselves and who purifies you? Our father in heaven. As it is said: 'And I will pour upon you pure water, and you will be purified of all your defilements, and from all your abominations I will purify you.' (Ezekiel 36:25). And it says: 'God is the hope of Israel.' (Jeremiah 17:13). Just as the reservoir of the ritual bath purifies the impure, so does the Holy One purify Israel. 'A fountain for gardens, a well of living waters and flowing streams from Lebanon.' (*Song of Songs* 4:15). 'And Adonai shall have washed away the turmoil of the daughters of Zion, and shall have purged the blood of Jerusalem from the midst thereof by a spirit of judgment and with a searing breath.' (Isaiah 4:4). 'And I will pour upon you pure water, and you will be purified of all your defilements, and from all your abominations I will purify you.'" (Ezekiel 36:25). (Mishna Yoma 8:9)

Before dressing the deceased:

I will greatly rejoice, my soul shall be joyful in my God, for God has clothed me with the garments of salvation; God has covered me with the robe of righteousness as a bridegroom puts on priestly glory and as the bride adorns herself with jewels. (Isaiah 61:10). And I said, "Let them set a pure headdress upon his head," and they set the pure headdress upon his head, and they clothed him with garments, and the angel of Adonai stood by. (Zechariah 3:5)

Other readings and various Hebrew chantings are included as part of the "standard" flow of the *taharah* liturgy. The reading is generally done in Hebrew, though many *chevrot* read both the English and the Hebrew, sometimes simultaneously, one aloud and the other chanted in the background. It is important that both the soul of the deceased and the team members in the room understand what is being read. If team members are not fluent in Hebrew, it is fine to read the text in English only. Additional Hebrew chanting,[16] *niggunim,* or humming may be used at any time to enhance the ritual, as long as it is respectful and appropriate text. These help with *kavanah* and enhance the beauty of this already-profound and involved ritual process. *Niggunim* are often used like background music while the team is busy doing tasks. They hold the energy and tone of the ritual between standard readings. Silence is also present and important during *taharah*. As with music, the silence between notes is often as important as the notes themselves.

The liturgy in *taharah* is used to manifest our intentions to midwife the soul of the deceased from this realm of existence (the *olam hazeh*) to another realm (the *olam haba*). Our *kavanah*, our intentions and focus of purpose, are the single most important elements of the performance of this ritual. We must go into the preparation room with the intent to do our best, to do no harm, to honor and aid the soul of the deceased, and to be kind and respectful. If we go in with this intent, we will always succeed in the performance of *taharah*.

מתכונן למוות

Practical Considerations I: Planning for Death

When we study death practices, we must also face death ourselves. It is part of the process. So I have included here some ideas to help plan for death—that is, for our own as well as the deaths of those we love. This list is not comprehensive but is intended to help lay the groundwork. As in all complex situations, it can help to consult others for guidance through the process.

Planning for Death: The Death Box

I studied with Rabbi Zalman Schachter-Shalomi (may his memory be a blessing) in the early 1990s as he was birthing his "spiritual eldering" work which later was published under the title *From Ageing to Sage-ing.* One tool he taught the class as we learned to face our mortality was what I call "the death box." In my home, it is an actual box: a cardboard file drawer about 6 inches by 14 inches by 18 inches with manila file folders, papers, and other items separated by dividers. This box should hold everything your loved ones might need when you die. So my wife and I have put in it all our insurance papers, our wills, a list of our computer passwords, bank accounts, and credit cards, etc. The intent is to save your family the trouble of having to dig that information out of the chaos that follows a death. In addition, it makes acting as your executor easier. Be sure to tell your family about this box, and show the members where you keep it. Then, once a year or so, update the information.

In this age of digital storage, it might be a good idea to have online copies of this material as well, sharing the files with loved ones so that if the box is unavailable or not found, or the spouse is out of town and unable to get the actual box, the desired death arrangements can be accessed when needed.

Ethical Wills

An ethical will is a way to pass on your values, what lessons you have learned, and what is important to you. It can be a letter, a dissertation, or a simple note—anything that conveys to your descendants what matters to you. This can be included in the "death box" or, more appropriately, given to your children while you are still alive. Every decade or so since I was forty, I have written a summary of my philosophy of life and given it to my children in the form of a letter. I was thrilled and amazed to discover that when our home was destroyed in a forest fire in 2000, one of the things my eleven-year-old daughter took with her as we were evacuated was the letter I had given her a few years earlier. These things have meaning beyond their words. They convey our love, our ideals, and a glimpse of who we truly are. Our children cherish these things.

Another teaching from Reb Zalman for those who share *Shabbat* is the idea of a "Shabbos letter," a note hidden under the dinner plate on Friday night, a kind of mini-ethical will, perhaps just a "thought for the week" from the larger volume of the entire philosophy of life you wish to pass on. Kids look forward to these, and appreciate them.

Any way you can pass on your values and the lessons you have learned about living should be given to your children, grandchildren, and even perhaps to siblings, so who you are will live on through your teachings. As you face your mortality, think about this, and create a legacy for future generations.

Wills and Advance Directives

A will contains your wishes regarding the disposition of your material and financial estate, including who should administer your estate. Although it can be prepared without a lawyer, you may wish to consult one, especially if your assets are substantial or the arrangements you want to make are complicated.

Another approach that often helps as you prepare your will is creating your estate as a legal trust, with you and your spouse as the trustees, and your children as the inheritors of the trust. If you do this, then when you die, nothing changes. There does not need to be an estate hearing or formal legal battle about who gets what. It's all part of the trust, and those left behind are automatically included as the new trustees. If you have a lawyer set this up, it is sure to be legally binding and a great gift to your children.

An advance directive (also known as a "durable power of attorney for health care") contains your wishes regarding end-of-life or emergency medical care. For instance, you may want to decide in advance whether "extraordinary measures" should be taken if you are found unconscious. These are complex and often disturbing issues to contemplate, and you may wish to consult a medical, legal, or pastoral professional for assistance in reaching decisions. Think about what kind of quality of life you might have, and if you want to be kept alive under such circumstances. Discuss this with your spouse. Perhaps jointly, you can come to decisions that make sense for your lifestyle.

Burial or Cremation?

Cremation is not supported by traditional Jewish practices. Rabbi Maurice Lamm states that, "Cremation is never permitted." Some of the reasons are historical, and others are based on the concept that the human body is like a holy vessel, similar to a no-longer-kosher *Torah* scroll, which should be treated with utmost respect because it is still sacred.

Jewish burial practices are based upon preserving the modesty and dignity of the deceased and treating her or his remains with utmost respect. The *taharah* process midwifes the now-disembodied soul from this world to the next. It honors the deceased and uplifts the soul. The placing of the body into the ground from which it came is the ultimate means to honor the holiness of the vessel that carried this soul with such integrity in life.

In modern cremation practices, the body is burned in a cardboard casket until only bone fragments are left. Most of the body is transformed into gaseous emissions into the air around the crematorium which then are spread on the winds. The remaining bones are made into powder in a mechanical grinder, and placed in a plastic bag which is put into a box or urn and given to the family as the "remains" of the loved one. Nothing in this process includes respect for the deceased. Not only is it devoid of human touch but it also is a mechanical process in which error may occur. Sometimes the remains of one person are mixed up with those of another, or mislabeled. The remnants from a previous cremation might be included in the next one. There are no guarantees that your loved one will return to you "pure," whatever that might mean under these circumstances. In addition, the soul of the deceased is shocked into moving on when the body is torched in this way.

Our tradition allows that it might take some time for the soul to integrate into the next world, an opportunity that being in the ground gives it to do this important after-life work.

In addition, when there is a grave and a burial, the mourning process can begin in earnest. The mourners will hear the shovelful of earth hit the casket. After this important step, the grave can be a place to which mourners can come for comfort and feelings of communion with the dead.

Jewish practices have lasted thousands of generations. There is a reason they have persevered and supported Jewish communities throughout the ages. It is obvious from my work with *taharah* that these practices are necessary and that we should choose to use them.

Preneed Funeral Arrangements

As you plan for your own death or the death of a loved one, some funeral arrangements can be planned ahead of time:

- Choosing a cemetery and buying a cemetery plot;
- Choosing a funeral home;
- Deciding if traditional Jewish burial practices will be followed;
- Writing down the Hebrew names, English names, and wishes of family members regarding their funeral arrangements

Once this is done, it is useful to create a list with phone numbers of the rabbi, funeral director, and other people to be contacted when a death occurs.

If you are affiliated with a synagogue, the rabbi or administrator may be able to help you with these arrangements, particularly if the synagogue has an associated cemetery. It may be appropriate to discuss all the options with the rabbi and funeral director, and make decisions ahead of time.

Organ Donation

It is important to plan ahead and make your wishes known if you wish to donate your organs. All branches of Judaism allow organ donation, although conditions may vary. Judaism teaches us that to save a life is the highest *mitzvah,* the most important thing we can do. So if donating your organs, tissues, or other body part will help save another person's life, Jewish teachings support this. Modern technology often allows more than one life to be helped through a single person's donations. Most states have a way to designate organ donation on your driver's license. Let your family know that you want to be a donor, and how much of your body you want to donate. You can donate internal organs, skin tissue, bone marrow, corneas of the eye, and sometimes other parts of the body. Organ donation does not impact whether *taharah* is performed. You can donate and still have a full Jewish burial.

Does the Family Want a Traditional Jewish Burial?

"Traditional" does not mean "Orthodox." In addition, neither the family nor the deceased needs to have been observant to have a traditional Jewish burial. All Jews deserve to be treated respectfully in death. Jewish burial ensures that the deceased will be treated with dignity and honor. The traditional Jewish burial usually includes but is not limited to having someone keep the deceased company between death and burial (*shmirah*), respectful preparation of the body for burial in a beautiful and sacred manner (*taharah*), dressing the deceased in plain but special burial clothes (*tachrichim*), placing the deceased into a simple wooden casket (*aron*), and burial of the casket into the earth, usually in a designated Jewish cemetery (*kevurah b'karka*). While burying the deceased in a casket is common in the United States, in other countries, such as Israel, it is perfectly acceptable to simply wrap the body in a burial sheet (and possibly a *tallit*), and place it in the grave.

Many communities have a *Chevrah Kadisha* to handle the arrangements between death and burial. If you are uncertain about these issues, a rabbi can help you understand them.

For a traditional Jewish *taharah,* the funeral home (on behalf of the *Chevrah Kadisha*) may ask for the Hebrew name of the deceased, including the Hebrew names of parents, for the *taharah*. They should also ask if the deceased has a *tallit* (prayer shawl) and whether you want the deceased buried in it. If the family wants but does not have one, the funeral home can generally provide it.

Cemeteries and Burial Sites

In choosing a cemetery and burial site, you may want to consider:

- Its location, especially if visiting the grave will be important to the family;
- The cemetery's religious affiliation (e.g., Orthodox, Reform, trans-denominational, etc.);
- Availability of plots for yourself and other family members;
- Cost.

Issues Around Status in Cemeteries

Each cemetery may have its own rules about who can be buried there. For instance, some allow burial of non-Jewish spouses, and others do not. Some cemeteries have separate areas for Orthodox and non-observant Jews.

What to Expect From Funeral Homes

Funeral home personnel are usually well trained in helping families during the time between death and burial. Many of them know how to work with Jewish families, and are extremely supportive and well prepared to help the *Chevrah Kadisha* perform the traditional practices of *shmirah* and *taharah*.

However, funeral homes are in business to make money. So it is important to understand that they are working hard to give good service for a reason. In addition, some personnel, even in funeral homes that frequently serve the Jewish community, may not fully understand Jewish death practices. Communicate clearly with the funeral home staff about what is desired for a deceased Jew. It helps if family members have communicated with each other so they can pres-

ent a single description of their needs to the funeral home. If problems arise between you and funeral home personnel, a rabbi usually can intercede on your behalf.

Caskets and Other Details

Traditional Jewish burial includes a simple wooden casket or no casket, no cremation, no embalming, preparation of the body by the *Chevrah Kadisha* rather than by funeral home personnel, and burial. Most funeral homes will work with you to meet these requirements if you are clear that this is what you want. If you do not know what to do, contact a rabbi or the local *Chevrah Kadisha* for guidance.

Some funeral homes may try to sell the family an expensive casket or other services because "your loved one is worth it!" This approach is not in keeping with Jewish tradition.

Information for the Funeral Home

To prepare the death certificate, the funeral home will often need to know the:

- Full legal name of the deceased, including the maiden name of a married woman using her husband's last name;
- Full English names of the parents of the deceased;
- Social Security number of the deceased;
- Citizenship of the deceased;
- Military status of the deceased;
- Place and date of birth of the deceased.

The funeral home will also need to know:

- Where will the deceased be buried? (If out of town, it will need the name of the out-of-town funeral home. If a traditional Jewish burial is desired, it will need to know whether the *Chevrah Kadisha* at the burial location has been contacted.)

- When is burial desired? Is it necessary to wait for out-of-town relatives to arrive?
- Will there be a service before burial? If so, who will be conducting the service and where?
- What should be done with any jewelry found on the deceased? Usually, this is returned to the family.

Practical Considerations II: When Death Occurs

What to Do

It is traditional for those present to recite *Baruch Dayan Ha-Emet* (Praised is the True Judge) immediately upon death (or if not present at the death, upon learning of it). Mourners also perform *k'riah* ("tearing" of a piece of clothing or a ribbon representing clothing), though this may be done at the time of the funeral or burial. Any of those present may assist with these steps:

- Close the eyes and mouth of the deceased and straighten the limbs;
- Cover the deceased with a sheet;
- Open the windows in the room where the deceased is lying. (If weather is an issue, open a window, then close it as needed.)
- Place a lighted candle near the head of the deceased (This is not done on *Shabbat;* on *Yom Tov,* kindle from a preexisting flame.)
- Cover the mirrors in the room where the deceased is lying. (If at home, cover all mirrors in the house.)

Before the body is picked up (usually by the funeral home), the family should take time to say goodbye to the deceased. Take as much time as you need; don't let yourself be rushed.

The deceased should not be left unattended, so immediately after death, *shmirah* (attending the deceased) begins. If the deceased died in a hospital or other medical setting, medical personnel may remove tubes, needles, etc.

Whom to Call

If you have made preneed arrangements, you likely will have a handy list of phone numbers for final arrangements. In any case, here is a simple list of steps to be taken:

- If the family is affiliated with a synagogue, contact the rabbi;

- If the family is unaffiliated, contact the funeral home;
- If a traditional Jewish burial is desired, contact (or have the rabbi contact) the *Chevrah Kadisha*, the sacred burial team that prepares the body for burial.
- Inform the important members of the deceased's family of the death, and the fact that arrangements are still being determined.

The funeral home will make arrangements for the body of the deceased to be picked up.

Note: If this is not a natural death (such as a violent one), or if the deceased is an organ or tissue donor, the process may differ, and authorities should be contacted. The funeral home personnel are usually equipped and trained to handle such situations.

What If We Don't Have a Burial Plot?

Usually consultation with a member of the clergy can facilitate purchase of an appropriate cemetery plot. This can be taken care of while making the other burial arrangements.

Who Owns This Death?

People generally deny the reality of death most of their lives. When death comes into a family, it can be a catalyst for chaos. Hence, it is important to:

- Plan for our own deaths;
- Plan for our parents' deaths; and
- Learn about death and funeral practices so we can be better prepared to handle the chaos.

Whose death is this? Someone must be the "champion" for this death to make sure everything happens the way the deceased would want it to. It should be "owned" by a friend or a member of the family of the deceased. That means someone must step up to take on the role of coordinator for this death, making decisions, communicating to other family members what's going on, making sure all the appropriate arrangements are made, and that the family's needs are taken care of. Sometimes people in the *Chevrah Kadisha* or a local rabbi or chaplain act as liaisons between the family of the deceased and the funeral home, helping guide the coordinator. If such help is not available, you must navigate the waters alone. You could turn to online websites, and might also contact experts by telephone through your local *chevrah* or through such organizations as Kavod v'Nichum. (See Appendix II).

What kinds of things need to be handled? For some starters:

- Will it be a traditional Jewish burial? If so, has the *Chevrah Kadisha* been notified? If not, why not, and is that a sufficient reason not to afford the deceased the respect and comfort of the traditional practices? Who should be contacted?
- What funeral home will be used? Who is the contact there?
- Where will the funeral and burial happen? If it is not where the body is, what arrangements must be made to ship the deceased to the appropriate town or city?

- When is the funeral? Will there be a funeral service and gravesite service, or just a single service? Is it timed to allow for arrival of family members who do not live where the service will be held?
- Who will the pallbearers be?
- Who will officiate? Does he or she know the family?
- Will there be a meal of consolation? If so, who will coordinate it?
- Will the family sit *shiva*? If so, where?
- Does the family wish to say *Kaddish* during *shiva*? If so, who is the contact to arrange services?

The Role of the Rabbi or Synagogue

The rabbi or synagogue representative can help in many ways. These people know what needs attention, such as contacting the most appropriate funeral home, contacting the *Chevrah Kadisha,* notifying the caring committee of the community to help the family, assisting with arrangements for burial and funeral service and transportation of the body as needed, providing *shiva* candles, making *shiva minyan* arrangements, and other things that help the family at this vulnerable time. The rabbi can also help counsel the family in a number of ways, including but not limited to helping them understand Jewish mourning practices, providing emotional support and guidance, and offering spiritual leadership.

What If I'm Not Affiliated?

Unaffiliated Jews deserve the same dignity and respect as all other Jews. In death, it is no differ-

ent. The only issue is whom should you contact since you don't belong to a synagogue or community. Many funeral homes maintain a list of rabbis who can help the family during this vulnerable time to make arrangements and appropriate decisions. If you cannot find a rabbi, contact a local synagogue.

What Does It All Cost?

In dealing with death, we cannot ignore the practical and real necessity to consider the costs. In today's world, many funeral homes have their own pricing arrangements, and there are few, if any, consistencies among the many choices available. The one exception to this chaos happens when the local Jewish community arranges a blanket contract with all the local funeral homes caring for Jewish families. Such contracts dictate an arranged price for a specific list of services. When possible, take advantage of such an arrangement. It usually will be cheaper, simplify all the choices, ensure a complete Jewish burial "package," eliminate confusion, and minimize the potential for mistakes.

The location of the funeral home will dictate many of the costs, since these vary across the country. Unless there is a contract with a funeral home, the choice of a casket will determine the total funeral cost. In the few areas where a Jewish funeral package has been negotiated, it includes the items below for about $2,000 to $3,000. The same funeral without an arranged package might cost as much as $5,000. Services usually included are:

- Transportation of the deceased from the place of death to the funeral home;
- Refrigeration;
- Use of the funeral home for the *Chevrah Kadisha;*
- *Shmirah*—the traditional vigil over the dead ;
- *Taharah*—the traditional ritual washing, purification, and dressing of the body;

- *Tachrichim*—simple white burial garments;
- A simple, unfinished wood coffin;
- Graveside, funeral home, or synagogue funeral service including a hearse for transportation.
- Securing a death certificate and newspaper notices.

About Kavod v'Nichum and the Gamliel Institute

Kavod v'Nichum (KvN) is Judaism's most comprehensive death-related education and training organization. Its mission is to support Jewish death and bereavement practices, including the traditions and values of honoring the dead (*kavod hamet*) and comforting the bereaved (*nichum aveilim*).

KvN advocates a return to an authentic and communal Jewish response toward illness, death, burial, and mourning. This includes strengthening individual and community efforts to organize caring communities and *Chevrah Kadisha* groups and also helping those groups adapt the traditions in new and meaningful ways. In addition, KvN works to protect bereaved families from commercial exploitation concerning funerals and burial.

Kavod v'Nichum began its work in November 2000 as a North American educational nonprofit. It was named one of North America's top fifty innovative Jewish organizations in the ninth annual *Slingshot Guide,* a resource guide to Jewish innovation, released in October 2013. Kavod v'Nichum's work, selected from among that of hundreds of finalists reviewed by eighty-three professionals with expertise in grantmaking and Jewish communal life, was seen as "timely, unique, and ubiquitous [in an] area of concern that is overlooked by most in our community." Organizations selected were evaluated on their innovative approach, the impact of their work, leadership in their sector, and effectiveness at achieving results.

Kavod v'Nichum sponsors annual international conferences, focused on *Chevrah Kadisha,* Jewish cemeteries, and other aspects of Jewish death practices, which have touched thousands of people. KvN's website (www.jewish-funerals.org) has extensive information on Jewish funerals, burial, and mourning. Further information about Jewish death-related practices and organizing a *Chevrah Kadisha* is also available at info@jewish-funerals.org.

KvN also sponsors the Gamliel Institute, a groundbreaking, world-class academic institution dedicated to educating and training leaders in the creation of a holistic death-related care continuum for local communities. The institute began in 2010 with the goals of deepening future leaders' Jewish knowledge and helping them experience the emotional, transformative, and spiritual aspects of *Chevrah Kadisha* work. The first full cohort of students completed the program in the spring of 2015, examining history and practice of the international *Chevrah Kadisha* movement through a study and travel mission to New York, Prague, and Israel. More information about Gamliel can be found on the KvN website.

Notes

1. The complex subject of when *minhag* becomes *halachah* is recognized and appreciated. The point in this text is that the practices in each community generally come from local custom handed down from generation to generation, and include all Jews.

2. Raphael, Simcha Paull. *Jewish Views of the Afterlife,* 2nd Edition, Rowman & Littlefield Publishers Inc., 2009, p. 418.

3. Jewish mysticism lists five aspects to our non-physical self, only one of which is called *neshamah.* I am using the term here to encapsulate the entirety of our nonphysical being. For clarity, the five levels of soul described by Isaac Luria, who lived from 1534–1572 and was a foremost teacher of Jewish mysticism, are *nefesh, ruach, neshamah, chayah,* and *yechidah.* These names emerge from rabbinic commentaries as early as first-century Palestine. See *Bereshit Rabbah* 14:9 and *Devarim Rabbah* 2:37.

4. One could also consider the modern scientific understanding that matter and energy cannot be created or destroyed but only converted from one form to another. In this case, the soul is energy changing forms.

5. Spitz, Elie Kaplan. *Does the Soul Survive? A Jewish Journey to Belief in Afterlife, Past Lives, and Living With Purpose.* Woodstock, VT: Jewish Lights Publishing, 2000, 2011, p. 24.

6. Ibid, pp. 13–21, 65–80.

7. Ibid, pp. 103–109.

8. This is the reading that begins, "Ruler of the Universe!" in the section on *The Power of Words —The Taharah Liturgy.*

9. This is from the Gamliel Institute's Course 1, Section 1.1. All Gamliel courses are available online and discuss all the subjects covered in significant depth. Information about Gamliel and Kavod v'Nichum can be found in Appendix II.

10. This section is my paraphrasing of the Gamliel Institute's materials for Course 1, Section 3, in which David Zinner discusses the history of *Chevrah Kadisha.*

11. Ibid. Course 1, Section 3.4.

12. Ibid. Course 1, Section 4.1.

13. Kelman, Stuart, and Fendel, Dan. *Chesed Shel Emet, The Truest Act of Kindness*. 3rd Edition, Berkeley, CA: EKS Publishing, 2013, pp. 2–5.

14. Ibid. p. 2.

15. Ibid. p. 3.

16. Hebrew chants to be included can be found in books by Richard A. Light and Rabbi Regina Sandler-Philips listed in the section titled For More Information.

אזכור

For More Information

There are many places to find information on Jewish death practices these days. Obviously the most prolific source is the internet. Below are some websites of particular interest and value in this regard, as well as ideas for contacts that might have, or help you to find, the guidance you seek.

Web References and Organizations

• Kavod v'Nichum. A North American non-profit educational organization focused on encouraging and assisting the organization of bereavement committees and *Chevrah Kadisha* groups to perform Jewish funeral, burial, and mourning practices; protect and shield bereaved families from exploitation; and provide information, education, and technical assistance. Its in-depth website provides resources for all aspects of Jewish death rituals and traditions (http://jewish-funerals.org/).

• The Gamliel Institute. This is a world-class institute of higher learning dedicated to comprehensive education related to Jewish death, dying, burial, and mourning. It is sponsored by Kavod v'Nichum (http://jewish-funerals.org/gamliel-institute).

• The National Association of Chevrah Kadisha.

This is an Orthodox resource for *Chevrot Kadisha, Rabbonim,* and the general public on all issues relating to Jewish burial. It provides support, information, education, and inspiration for all those involved with and seeking information about traditional Jewish burial (http://www.nasck.org/index.htm).

• The National Association of Jewish Chaplains. The website of this worldwide organization is the address for Jewish chaplaincy expertise promoting the highest standards of training, certification, and delivery of care (http://www.najc.org/about/mission).

• The National Association for Home Care and Hospice. This is the largest U.S. trade association representing the interests and concerns of home-care agencies, hospices, and home-care aide organizations (http://www.nahc.org/).

• Hospice Association of America. This national organization is devoted to promoting hospice as the primary method of caring for the terminally ill (http://www.nahc.org/haa/).

• Jewish Cemetery Association of North America. This is the central organization devoted to the preservation, sanctity, and continuity of Jewish cemeteries (http://www.jcana.org/).

Conferences

Kavod v'Nichum sponsors annual Chevrah Kadisha and Jewish cemetery conferences every year, usually in the early summer, with attendees from all over the U.S. and parts of Canada, and in recent years from England and Australia as well. These conferences include sessions on *taharah*, *Chevrah Kadisha*, chaplaincy, cemetery, education, community inclusiveness, and dealing with modern dilemmas related to Jewish death in today's society. The program changes each year. More information is available at the Kavod website.

Books

- Epstein, Mosha. *Taharah Manual of Practices, Including Halacha Decisions of Hagaon Harav Moshe Feinstein, zt'l.* Bridgeport, CT: 1995.
- Goodman, Arnold M. *A Plain Pine Box.* NY: KTAV Publishing, 1981.
- Kelman, Stuart, and Fendel, Dan. *Chesed Shel Emet, The Truest Act of Kindness.* 3rd Edition, Berkeley, CA: EKS Publishing, 2013.
- Kelman, Stuart, and Fendel, Dan. *Nichum Aveilim,* Berkeley, CA: EKS Publishing, 2015.
- Lamm, Maurice. *The Jewish Way in Death and Mourning.* N.Y: Jonathan David, 1969.
- Library of the Jewish Theological Seminary of America. *From This World to the Next.* NY: JTS, 1999.
- Light, Richard A. *Final Kindness: Honoring K'rovei Yisrael, Burial Preparation of Non-Jews Who Are Part of the Jewish Community.* Santa Fe, NM: Chevrah Kadisha of Northern New Mexico, 2013.
- Light, Richard A. *To Midwife A Soul, Guidelines for Performing Taharah.* 4th Edition, Santa Fe, N.M.: Chevrah Kadisha of Northern New Mexico, 2013.
- Rabinowicz, Tzvi. *A Guide to Life, Jewish Laws, and Customs of Mourning.* Northvale, NJ: Jason Aronson Inc., 1989.
- Raphael, Simcha Paull. *Jewish Views of the Afterlife.* 2nd Edition, Lanham, MD: Roman and Littlefield Publishers Inc., 2004.
- Sandler-Phillips, Regina L. *PSJC Hevra Kadisha Taharah Manual.* 2nd Edition, Brooklyn, NY: Park Slope Jewish Center, 2009.
- Schlingenbaum, Yechezkel. *Taharah Guide, Prepared for the New Haven Chevrah Kadisha.* New Haven, CT: 1991.
- Spitz, Elie Kaplan. *Does the Soul Survive? A Jewish Journey to Belief in Afterlife, Past Lives, and Living with Purpose.* Woodstock, VT: Jewish Lights Publishing, 2000, 2011.
- Wolfson, Ron. *A Time to Mourn, A Time to Comfort.* Woodstock, VT: Jewish Lights Publishing, 1996.

About the Author and Photographer

Author Richard A. Light has been teaching spiritual development in various ways for more than thirty years, and has been studying and practicing meditation for more than forty years. He also teaches backpacking, rock climbing, and other outdoor skills. He is a leader in the community of those who prepare Jewish bodies for burial, has published three books on the subject, and for eighteen years was president of a local *Chevrah Kadisha* he started in 1996. He is a vice president of the North American educational organization Kavod v'Nichum (Honor and Comfort), and continues to teach and raise awareness about Jewish death and burial practices at the local, state, and national levels.

Photographer Thea Rose Light grew up amid the high desert landscapes of northern New Mexico. She is involved with many types of art and media, though mainly photography and a sketchbook. She received her BFA in photography from the Santa Fe University of Art and Design in 2011.

Other Books by Richard A. Light

To Midwife a Soul: Guidelines for Performing *Taharah, Expanded Fourth Edition, with Chants by Rabbi Shefa Gold*

This manual is a guide for those who perform the holy ritual of *taharah,* preparation of Jewish deceased for burial. Written for the Chevrah Kadisha of Northern New Mexico, which includes six shuls differing extensively in their levels of observance, it is intended for use by any community. It is for all Jews. Earlier editions have been popular in the U.S. since the early 2000s, and in England since 2008.

The 4th Edition is specially formatted for ease of use in the *taharah* room as well as for education and teaching. Music has long been known to enhance the beauty and *kavanah* of the ritual. This edition is unique in that it includes the musical chanting notations of the Hebrew chant scholar, Rabbi Shefa Gold. An essential resource to those who help midwife souls from this world to the next, the book is a beautiful contribution to the field.

ISBN 978-1-489574-63-3

Final Kindness: Honoring *K'rovei Yisrael,* Burial Preparation for Non-Jews Who Are Part of the Jewish Community

In today's modern Jewish society, we are faced with an increasing number of interfaith families in which one spouse is Jewish and the other is not. If the Jewish member of the couple asks that his or her non-Jewish spouse be buried as a Jew, a dilemma arises. How does one prepare a non-Jew for burial using Jewish traditions? Many *chevrot* and synagogues simply deny the request, stating that Jewish practices are only for Jews. Yet with so many families now expressing interest in this, it is time to create a new ritual. This book is the first of its kind in the field of Jewish death rituals, and extends the scope of the current Jewish umbrella under which our dead are respectfully prepared for burial. Every *Chevrah Kadisha* needs to be ready to handle the changing times of today's world, and thus, every community in which there are mixed-religion marriages needs this manual.

ISBN 978-1-484880-16-6

Exploring the Soul of *Taharah,* coauthored with Rabbi Avivah W. Erlick

Judaism's rituals for responding to death are ancient and deep; beautiful, mysterious, and misunderstood; filled with meaning, wonder, and kindness; and as diverse as are the communities of Jews the world over. One of the central elements of these traditions is the ritual known as *taharah,* the long-established cultural and religious ceremony of ablution by which the Jewish people prepare their dead for disposition.

Created as a collaborative effort in preparation for a conference session, this book examines what is really necessary for a washing ceremony to be called *taharah,* what is necessary for it to be considered Jewish, and what differences matter between traditional methods of performing this sacred ritual and emerging variations adopted to accommodate the needs of modern Western culture.

When is a *taharah* a *taharah*? How shall we, as Jews, show kindness and honor to our dead, support the soul of the deceased in transition, and at the same time, comfort and respect those who must carry on without them? This book examines these questions and the essence of this amazing ritual to seek the "soul of *taharah,*" to understand what it is that makes it work.

As David Zinner, executive director of *Kavod v'Nichum,* wrote: "Destined to become a defining work in the *chevrah kadisha* field, [this book] extends the concepts of hospice into a Jewish context, and has the potential to radically alter and improve the way that contemporary Jews handle traditional death practices. It may facilitate the return to a more-authentic form of the *chevrah kadisha* that is not dependent upon twentieth-century funeral homes."

ISBN 978-1-508412-36-6

מפתח

Index